D0961113

Virtues
of
Family Life

WILLIAM J. BENNETT

W PUBLISHING GROUP

www.wpublishinggroup.com

A Division of Thomas Nelson, Inc.
www.ThomasNelson.com

Virtues of Family Life

© 2001 W Publishing Group

Published by W Publishing Group, a Division of Thomas Nelson, Inc., P.O. Box 141000, Nashville, Tennessee 37214. All rights reserved. No portion of this book may be reproduced, stored in a retrieval system, or transmitted in any form or by any means—electronic, mechanical, photocopy, recording, or any other—except for brief quotations in printed reviews, without the prior permission of the publisher.

Material in this book is compiled from both *The Book of Virtues* and *The Moral Compass* by William J. Bennett, copyright © 1993 by William J Bennett and copyright © 1996 by William J. Bennett.

Published by arrangement with Simon & Shuster, Inc.

Library of Congress Cataloging-in-Publication Data

ISBN 0–8499–1716–6

Printed in the United States of America

01 02 03 04 05 06 07 08 09 — 9 8 7 6 5 4 3 2 1

Contents

Introduction

WILLIAM J. BENNETT

F amily, along with church, is an indispensable institution. It gives us our basic moral sense. The transmission of virtues is one important reason for a home, and attention to the virtues is one of the important ties that bind a family together. "It is the peculiarity of man, in comparison with the rest of the animal world," Aristotle wrote, "that he alone possesses a perception of good and evil, of the just and the unjust, and of other similar qualities; and it is association in these things which makes a family."

Home is the place where children receive their first instruction in the virtues, the moral training ground where right is separated from wrong. It is the place where parents do the most important teaching of all. Character takes shape under the dos and don'ts offered around the house. Equally important, a family's moral sense thrives or withers under the influence of examples set by mother, father, sisters, and brothers.

In this book you will find some of the lessons we can learn from our families. You'll find family members helping each other along, and looking toward each other for help. You'll find siblings showing what "brotherhood" and "sisterhood" really mean. You'll see what virtues like loyalty and courage and perseverance mean to families, and how the love of family can overcome any number of obstacles.

These virtues stay with us, of course, long after we leave our first homes. In our affections and memories, they remain a part of us, often the most cherished part. "Where shall a man find sweetness to surpass his own home and parents?" Odysseus asks in Homer's *Odyssey*. "In far lands he shall not, though he find a house of gold." The early experiences of home become a moral compass point, guiding and instructing us for the rest of life's journey.

In one sense, the moral journey that begins with leaving home is the search for opportunities to offer others the same nurture and love we received in our own childhood. The best memories of home become ideals we seek to re-create in our later lives and in the new lives we shepherd into the world. We build our own homes, offer our own lessons, nurture our own children in the strength and knowledge we once gained beside the first warm hearth of home.

Of course, no family is perfect. Home can be the place where we get our first look at vices as well as virtues. And, unfortunately, some homes are simply not good places—not all homes are havens, not all hearths have a warm glow. But *all* homes teach lessons, even if they are the wrong kind of lessons. And so even though many homes fall short of the best ones we find in these pages, the stories here are no less valuable because they give us all something at which to aim. They remind us of the kind of conditions families need and the attention our loved ones deserve. We set these examples before our eyes to keep raising our sights and efforts.

About Angels

LAURA E. RICHARDS

Here is a story about a true guardian angel, the kind who watches over us from the moment we come into the world.

"Mother," said the child, "are there really angels?"

"The Good Book says so," said the mother.

"Yes," said the child. "I have seen the picture. But did you ever see one, Mother?"

"I think I have," said the mother, "but she was not dressed like the picture."

"I am going to find one!" said the child. "I am going to run along the road, miles, and miles, and miles, until I find an angel."

"That will be a good plan!" said the mother. "And I will go with you, for you are too little to run far alone."

"I am not little anymore!" said the child. "I have trousers; I am big."

"So you are!" said the mother. "I forgot. But it is a fine day, and I should like the walk."

"But you walk so slowly, with your lame foot."

"I can walk faster than you think!" said the mother.

So they started, the child leaping and running, and the mother stepping out so bravely with her lame foot that the child soon forgot about it.

The child danced on ahead, and presently he saw a chariot coming toward him, drawn by a prancing white horse. In the chariot sat a splendid lady in velvet and furs, with white plumes waving above her dark hair. As she moved in her seat, she flashed with jewels and gold, but her eyes were brighter than her diamonds.

"Are you an angel?" asked the child, running up beside the chariot.

The lady made no reply, but stared coldly at the child. Then she spoke a word to her coachman, and he flicked his whip, and the chariot rolled away swiftly in a cloud of dust, and disappeared.

The dust filled the child's eyes and mouth, and made him choke and sneeze. He gasped for breath, and rubbed his eyes; but presently his mother came up, and wiped away the dust with her blue gingham apron.

"That was not an angel!" said the child.

"No, indeed!" said the mother. "Nothing like one!"

The child danced on again, leaping and running from side to side of the road, and the mother followed as best she might.

By and by the child met a most beautiful maiden, clad in a white dress. Her eyes were like blue stars, and the blushes came and went in her face like roses looking through snow.

"I am sure you must be an angel!" cried the child.

The maiden blushed more sweetly than before. "You dear little child!" she cried. "Someone else said that, only last evening. Do I really look like an angel?"

"You *are* an angel!" said the child.

The maiden took him up in her arms and kissed him, and held him tenderly.

"You are the dearest little thing I ever saw!" she said. "Tell me what makes you think so!" But suddenly her face changed.

"Oh!" she cried. "There he is, coming to meet me! And you have soiled my white dress with your dusty shoes, and pulled my hair all awry. Run away, child, and go home to your mother!"

She set the child down, not unkindly, but so hastily that he stumbled and fell; but she did not see that, for she was hastening forward to meet her lover, who was coming along the road. (Now if the maiden had only known, he thought her twice as lovely with the child in her arms; but she did not know.)

The child lay in the dusty road and sobbed, till his mother came along and picked him up, and wiped away the tears with her blue gingham apron.

"I don't believe that was an angel, after all," he said.

"No!" said the mother. "But she may be one someday. She is young yet."

"I am tired!" said the child. "Will you carry me home, Mother?"

"Why, yes!" said the mother. "That is what I came for."

The child put his arms 'round his mother's neck and she held him tight and trudged along the road, singing the song he liked best.

Suddenly he looked up in her face.

"Mother," he said. "I don't suppose *you* could be an angel, could you?"

"Oh, what a foolish child!" said the mother. "Who ever heard of an angel in a blue gingham apron?" And she went on singing, and stepped out so bravely on her lame foot that no one would ever have known she was lame.

Beautiful Hands

ADAPTED FROM LAWTON B. EVANS

Happy homes need helpful hands.

S ome young girls were talking by the brook, boasting of their beautiful hands. One of them dipped her hands in the sparkling water and the drops looked like diamonds falling from her palms.

"See what beautiful hands I have! The water runs from them like precious jewels," said she, and held up her hands for the others to admire. They were very soft and white, for she had never done anything but wash them in clear, cold water.

Another one of them ran to get some strawberries and crushed them in her palms. The juice ran through her fingers like wine from a wine press until her fingers were as pink as the sunrise in the early morning.

"See what beautiful hands I have! The strawberry juice runs over them like wine," said she, and she held up her hands for the others to admire. They were very pink and soft, for she had never done anything but wash them in strawberry juice every morning.

Another one gathered some violets and crushed the flowers in her hands until they smelled like perfume.

"See what beautiful hands I have! They smell like violets in the deep woods in the springtime," said she, and she held up her hands for the others to admire. They were very soft and white, for she had never done anything but wash them in violets every morning.

The fourth girl did not show her hands but held them in her lap. An old woman came down the road and stopped before the girls. They all showed her their hands and asked her which were the most beautiful. She shook her head at each one and then asked to see the hands of the last girl, who held hers in her lap. The last girl raised her hands timidly for the old woman to see.

"Oh, these hands are clean, indeed," said the old woman, "but they are hard from toil. These hands have been helping Mother and Father dry the dishes, and sweep the floor, and wash the windows, and weed the garden. These hands have been taking care of the baby, and carrying hot tea to Grandma, and showing little brother how to build his blocks and fly his kite. Yes, these hands have been busy making the house a happy home, full of love and care."

Then the old woman fumbled in her pocket and brought out a ring set with diamonds, with rubies redder than strawberries, and turquoise bluer than violets.

"Here, wear this ring, my child. You deserve the prize for the most beautiful hands, for they have been the most helpful."

And the old woman vanished, leaving the four girls still sitting by the brook.

Cain and Abel

RETOLD BY JESSE LYMAN HURLBUT

Here, according to the Bible, is the story of the first murder. Just as God sought out Adam and Eve in the Garden of Eden when they fell ("What is this that thou hast done?"), he seeks Cain after Abel's death. Just as Adam and Eve tried to avoid blame ("The serpent beguiled me"), Cain denies his crime. Whether or not one believes in original sin or divine reconciliation, there is certainly no denying our age-old struggle to accept responsibility for our own trespasses.

Adam and Eve went out into the world to live and to work. For a time they were all alone, but after a while God gave them a little child of their own, the first baby that ever came into the world. Eve named him Cain; and after a time another baby came, whom she named Abel.

When the two boys grew up, they worked, as their father worked before them. Cain chose to work in the fields, and to raise grain and fruits. Abel had a flock of sheep and became a shepherd.

While Adam and Eve were living in the Garden of Eden, they could talk with God, and hear God's voice speaking to them. But now that they were out in the world, they could no longer talk with God freely, as before. So when they came to God, they built an altar of stones heaped up, and upon it they laid something as a gift to God, and burned it, to show that it was not their own, but was given to God, Whom they could not see. Then before the altar they made their prayer to God, and asked God to forgive their sins—all that they had done that was wrong—and prayed God to bless them and do good to them.

Each of these brothers, Cain and Abel, offered upon the altar to God his own gift. Cain brought the fruits and the grain which he had grown. And Abel brought a sheep from his flock, and killed it and burned it upon the altar. For some reason God was pleased with Abel and his offering, but was not pleased with Cain and his offering. Perhaps Cain's heart was not right when he came before God.

And God showed that He was not pleased with Cain, and Cain, instead of being sorry for his sin, and asking God to forgive him, was very angry with God, and angry also toward his brother Abel. When they were out in the field together, Cain struck his brother Abel and killed him. So the first baby in the world grew up to be the murderer of his own brother.

And the Lord said to Cain, "Where is Abel your brother?"

And Cain answered, "I do not know. Am I my brother's keeper?"

Then the Lord said to Cain, "What is this that you have done? Your brother's blood is like a voice crying to Me from the ground. Do you see how the ground has opened, like a mouth, to drink your brother's blood? As long as you live, you shall be under God's curse for the murder of your brother. You shall wander over the earth, and shall never find a home, because you have done this wicked deed."

And Cain said to the Lord, "My punishment is greater than I can bear. Thou hast driven me out from among men, and Thou hast hid Thy face from me. If any man finds me he will kill me, because I shall be alone, and no one will be my friend."

And God said to Cain, "If anyone harms Cain, he shall be punished for it." And the Lord God placed a mark on Cain, so that whoever met him should know him, and should know also that God had forbidden any man to harm him. Then Cain and his wife went away from Adam's home, to live in a place by themselves, and there they had children. And Cain's family built a city in that land, and Cain named the city after his first child, whom he had called Enoch.

The Children's Hour

HENRY WADSWORTH LONGFELLOW

Every home should have at least one Children's Hour every evening.

Between the dark and the daylight,
When the night is beginning to lower,
Comes a pause in the day's occupations,
That is known as the Children's Hour.

I hear in the chamber above me
The patter of little feet,
The sound of a door that is opened,
And voices soft and sweet.

From my study I see in the lamplight,
Descending the broad hall stair,
Grave Alice, and laughing Allegra,
And Edith with golden hair.

A whisper, and then a silence:
Yet I know by their merry eyes
They are plotting and planning together
To take me by surprise.

A sudden rush from the stairway,
A sudden raid from the hall!
By three doors left unguarded
They enter my castle wall!

They climb up into my turret
O'er the arms and back of my chair;
If I try to escape, they surround me;
They seem to be everywhere.

They almost devour me with kisses,
Their arms about me entwine,
Till I think of the Bishop of Bingen
In his Mouse Tower on the Rhine!

Do you think, O blue-eyed banditti,
Because you have scaled the wall,
Such an old mustache as I am
Is not a match for you all!

I have you fast in my fortress,
And will not let you depart,
But put you down into the dungeon
In the round-tower of my heart.

And there will I keep you forever,
Yes, forever and a day,
Till the walls shall crumble to ruin,
And molder in dust away!

The Drover's Wife

HENRY LAWSON

Australian Henry Lawson (1867–1922) wrote this story of a remark-able woman holding her home together while her husband is driving sheep to market. It is the story of a family that survives only because it is fortunate enough to have a mother who knows how to persevere.

The two-roomed house is built of round timber, slabs, and stringy bark, and floored with split slabs. A big bark kitchen standing at one end is larger than the house itself, veranda included.

Bush all around—bush with no horizon, for the country is flat. No ranges in the distance. The bush consists of stunted, rotten native apple trees. No undergrowth. Nothing to relieve the eye save the darker green of a few she-oaks which are sighing above the narrow, almost waterless creek. Nineteen miles to the nearest sign of civilization—a shanty on the main road.

The drover, an ex-squatter, is away with sheep. His wife and children are left here alone.

Four ragged, dried-up-looking children are playing about the house. Suddenly one of them yells: "Snake! Mother, here's a snake!"

The gaunt, sun-browned bushwoman dashes from the kitchen, snatches her baby from the ground, holds it on her left hip, and reaches for a stick.

"Where is it?"

"Here! Gone into the wood heap!" yells the eldest boy—a sharp-faced urchin of eleven. "Stop there, Mother! I'll have him. Stand back! I'll have the beggar!"

"Tommy, come here, or you'll be bit. Come here at once when I tell you, you little wretch!"

The youngster comes reluctantly, carrying a stick bigger than himself. Then he yells, triumphantly: "There it goes—under the house!" and darts away with club uplifted. At the same time the big, black, yellow-eyed dog-of-all-breeds, who has shown the wildest interest in the proceedings, breaks his chain and rushes after that snake. He is a moment late, however, and his nose reaches the crack in the slabs just as the end of its tail disappears. Almost at the same moment the boy's club comes down and skins the aforesaid nose. Alligator takes small notice of this, and proceeds to undermine the building; but he is subdued after a struggle and chained up. They cannot afford to lose him.

The drover's wife makes the children stand together near the doghouse while she watches for the snake. She gets two small dishes of milk and sets them down near the wall to tempt it to come out; but an hour goes by and it does not show itself.

It is near sunset, and a thunderstorm is coming. The children must be brought inside. She will not take them into the house, for she knows the snake is there, and may at any moment come up through a crack in the rough slab floor: So she carries several armfuls of firewood into the kitchen, and then takes the children there. The kitchen has no floor—or, rather an earthen one—called a "ground floor" in this part of the bush. There is a large, roughly made table in the center of the place. She brings the children in, and makes them get on this table. They are two boys and two girls—mere babies. She gives them some supper, and then, before it gets dark, she goes into the house, and snatches up some pillows and bedclothes—expecting to see or lay her hand on the snake any minute. She makes a bed on the kitchen table for the children, and sits down beside it to watch all night.

She has an eye on the corner, and a green sapling club laid in readiness on the dresser by her side; also her sewing basket and a copy of the *Young Ladies' Journal*. She has brought the dog into the room.

Tommy turns in, under protest, but says he'll lie awake all night and smash that blinded snake.

His mother asks him how many times she has told him not to swear.

He has his club with him under the bedclothes, and Jacky protests: "Mummy! Tommy's skinnin' me alive wif his club. Make him take it out."

Tommy: "Shet up, you little—! D'yer want to be bit with the snake?"

Jacky shuts up.

"If yer bit," says Tommy, after a pause, "you'll swell up, an' smell, an' turn red an' green an' blue all over till yer bust. Won't he, Mother?"

"Now then, don't frighten the child. Go to sleep," she says.

The two younger children go to sleep, and now and then Jacky complains of being "skeezed." More room is made for him.

Presently Tommy says: "Mother! Listen to them (adjective) little possums. I'd like to screw their blanky necks."

And Jacky protests drowsily.

"But they don't hurt us, the little blanks!"

Mother: "There, I told you you'd teach Jacky to swear." But the remark makes her smile. Jacky goes to sleep.

Presently Tommy asks: "Mother! Do you think they'll ever extricate the (adjective) kangaroo?"

"Lord! How am I to know, child? Go to sleep."

"Will you wake me if the snake comes out?"

"Yes. Go to sleep."

Near midnight. The children are all asleep and she sits there still, sewing and reading by turns. From time to time she glances 'round the floor and wall plate, and whenever she hears a noise she reaches for the stick. The thunderstorm comes on, and the wind, rushing through the cracks in the slab wall, threatens to blow out her candle. She places it on a sheltered part of the dresser and fixes up a newspaper to protect it. At every flash of lightning the cracks between the slabs gleam like polished silver. The thunder rolls, and the rain comes down in torrents.

Alligator lies at full length on the floor, with his eyes turned toward the partition. She knows by this that the snake is there. There are large cracks in that wall opening under the floor of the house.

She is not a coward, but recent events have shaken her nerves. A little son of her brother-in-law was lately bitten by a snake, and died. Besides, she has not heard from her husband for six months, and is anxious about him.

He was a drover, and started squatting here when they were married. The drought of 18— ruined him. He had to sacrifice the remnant of his flock and go droving again. He intends to move his family into the nearest town when he comes back, and, in the meantime, his brother, who keeps a shanty on the main road, comes over about once a month with provisions. The wife has still a couple of cows, one horse, and a few sheep. The brother-in-law kills one of the latter occasionally, gives her what she needs of it, and takes the rest in return for other provisions.

She is used to being left alone. She once lived like this for eighteen months. As a girl she built the usual castles in the air; but all her girlish hopes and aspirations have long been dead. She finds all the excitement and recreation she needs in the *Young Ladies' Journal,* and—Heaven help her!—takes a pleasure in the fashion plates.

Her husband is an Australian, and so is she. He is careless, but a good enough husband. If he had the means he would take her to the city and keep her there like a princess. They are used to being apart, or at least she is. "No use fretting," she says. He may forget sometimes that he is married; but if he has a good check when he comes back he will give most of it to her. When he had money he took her to the city several times—hired a railway sleeping compartment, and put up at the best hotels. He also bought her a buggy, but they had to sacrifice that along with the rest.

The last two children were born in the bush—one while her husband was bringing a drunken doctor, by force, to attend to her. She was alone on this occasion, and very weak. She had been ill with a fever. She prayed to God to send her assistance. God sent Black Mary—the "whitest" gin in all the land. Or, at least, God sent King Jimmy first, and he sent Black Mary. He put his black face round the doorpost, took in the situation at a glance, and said cheerfully: "All right, missus—I bring my old woman, she down along a creek."

One of the children died while she was here alone. She rode nineteen miles for assistance, carrying the dead child.

It must be near one or two o'clock. The fire is burning low. Alligator lies with his head resting on his paws, and watches the wall. He is not a very beautiful dog, and the light shows numerous old wounds where the hair will not grow. He is afraid of nothing on the face of the earth or under it. He will tackle a bullock as readily as he will tackle a flea. He hates all other dogs—except kangaroo dogs—and has a marked dislike to friends or relations of the family. They seldom call, however. He sometimes makes friends with strangers. He hates snakes and has killed many, but he will be bitten someday and die; most snake dogs end that way.

Now and then the bushwoman lays down her work and watches, and listens, and thinks. She thinks of things in her own life, for there is little else to think about.

The rain will make the grass grow, and this reminds her how she fought a bushfire once while her husband was away. The grass was long, and very dry, and the fire threatened to burn her out. She put on an old pair of her husband's trousers and beat out the flames with a green bough, till great drops of sooty perspiration stood out on her forehead and ran in streaks down her blackened arms. The sight of his mother in trousers greatly amused Tommy, who worked like a little hero by her side, but the terrified baby howled lustily for his "mummy." The fire would have mastered her but for four excited bushmen who arrived in the nick of time. It was a mixed-up affair all 'round; when she went to take up the baby he screamed and struggled convulsively, thinking it was a "blackman"; and Alligator, trusting more to the child's sense than his own instinct, charged furiously, and (being old and slightly deaf) did not in his excitement at first recognize his mistress's voice, but continued to hang on to the moleskins until choked off by Tommy with a saddle strap. The dog's sorrow for his blunder, and his anxiety to let it be known that it was all a mistake, was as evident as his ragged tail and twelve-inch grin could make it. It was a glorious time for the boys; a day to look back to, and talk about, and laugh over for many years.

She thinks how she fought a flood during her husband's absence. She stood for hours in the drenching downpour, and dug an overflow gutter to save the dam across the creek. But she could not save it. There are things that a bushwoman cannot do. Next morning the dam was broken, and her heart was nearly broken, too, for she thought how her husband would feel when he came home and saw the result of years of labor swept away. She cried then.

She also fought the pleuropneumonia—dosed and bled the few remaining cattle, and wept again when her two best cows died.

Again, she fought a mad bullock that besieged the house for a day. She made bullets and fired at him through cracks in the slabs with an old shotgun. He was dead in the morning. She skinned him and got seventeen-and-sixpence for the hide.

She also fights the crows and eagles that have designs on her chickens. Her plan of campaign is very original. The children cry "Crows, Mother!" and she rushes out and aims a broomstick at the birds as though it were a gun, and says, "Bung!" The crows leave in a hurry; they are cunning, but a woman's cunning is greater.

Occasionally a bushman in the horrors, or a villainous-looking sundowner, comes and nearly scares the life out of her. She generally tells the suspicious-looking stranger that her husband and two sons are at work below the dam, or over at the yard, for he always cunningly inquires for the boss.

Only last week a gallows-faced swagman—having satisfied himself that there were no men on the place—threw his swag down on the veranda, and demanded tucker. She gave him something to eat; then he expressed his intention of staying for the night. It was sundown then. She got a batten from the sofa, loosened the dog, and confronted the stranger, holding the batten in one hand and the dog's collar with the other. "Now you go!" she said. He looked at her and at the dog, said, "All right, mum," in a cringing tone, and left. She was a determined-looking woman, and Alligator's yellow eyes glared unpleasantly—besides, the dog's chawing-up apparatus greatly resembled that of the reptile he was named after.

She has few pleasures to think of as she sits here alone by the fire, on guard against a snake. All days are much the same to her; but on Sunday afternoon she dresses herself, tidies the children, smartens up baby, and goes for a lonely walk along the bush track, pushing an old perambulator in front of her. She does this every Sunday. She takes as much care to make herself and the children look smart as she would if she were going to do the block in the city. There is nothing to see, however, and not a soul to meet. You might walk twenty miles along this track without being able to fix a point in your mind, unless you are a bushman. This is because of the everlasting, maddening sameness of the stunted trees—that monotony which makes a man long to break away and travel as far as trains can go, and sail as far as ships can sail—and farther.

But this bushwoman is used to the loneliness of it. As a girl-wife she hated it, and now she would feel strange away from it.

She is glad when her husband returns, but she does not gush or make a fuss about it. She gets him something good to eat, and tidies up the children.

She seems contented with her lot. She loves her children, but has no time to show it. She seems harsh to them. Her surroundings are not favorable to the development of the "womanly" or sentimental side of nature.

———————

It must be near morning now; but the clock is in the dwelling house. Her candle is nearly done, she forgot that she was out of candles. Some more wood must be got to keep the fire up, and so she shuts the dog inside and hurries 'round to the wood heap. The rain has cleared off. She seizes a stick, pulls it out, and—crash! the whole pile collapses.

Yesterday she bargained with a stray black fellow to bring her some wood, and while he was at work she went in search of a missing cow. She was absent an hour or so, and the native black made good use of his time. On her return she was so astonished to see a good heap of wood by the chimney that she gave him an extra fig of tobacco, and praised him for not being lazy. He thanked her, and left with head erect and chest well out. He was the last of his tribe and a king; but he had built that wood heap hollow.

She is hurt now, and tears spring to her eyes as she sits down again by the table. She takes up a handkerchief to wipe the tears away, but pokes her eyes with her bare fingers instead. The handkerchief is full of holes, and she finds that she has put her thumb through one, and her forefinger through another.

This makes her laugh, to the surprise of the dog. She has a keen, very keen, sense of the ridiculous; and sometime or other she will amuse bushmen with the story.

She had been amused before like that. One day she sat down "to have a good cry," as she said—and the old cat rubbed against her dress and "cried, too." Then she had to laugh.

———————

It must be near daylight now. The room is very close and hot because of the fire. Alligator still watches the wall from time to time. Suddenly he becomes greatly interested; he draws himself a few inches nearer the partition, and a thrill runs through his body. The hair on the back of his neck begins to bristle, and the battle light is in his yellow eyes. She knows what this means, and lays her hand on the stick. The lower end of one of the partition slabs has a large crack on both sides. An evil pair of small bright bead-like eyes glisten at one of these holes. The snake— a black one—comes slowly out, about a foot, and moves its head up and down. The dog lies still, and the woman sits as one fascinated. The snake comes out a foot farther. She lifts her stick, and the reptile, as though suddenly aware of danger, sticks his head in through the crack on the other side of the slab, and hurries to get his tail 'round after him. Alligator springs, and his jaws come together with a snap. He misses, for his nose is large, and the snake's body close down in the angle formed by the slabs and the floor. He snaps again as the tail comes 'round. He has the snake now, and tugs it out eighteen inches. Thud, thud, comes the woman's club on the ground. Alligator pulls again. Thud, thud. Alligator gives another pull and he has the snake out—a black brute, five feet long. The head rises to dart about, but the dog has the enemy close to the neck. He is a big, heavy dog, but quick as a terrier. He shakes the snake as though he felt the original curse in common with mankind. The eldest boy wakes up, seizes his stick, and tries to get out of bed, but his mother forces him back with a grip of iron. Thud, thud—the snake's back is broken in several places. Thud, thud—its head is crushed, and Alligator's nose skinned again.

She lifts the mangled reptile on the point of her stick, carries it to the fire, and throws it in; then piles on the wood and watches the snake burn. The boy and dog watch, too. She lays her hand on the dog's head, and all the fierce, angry light dies out of his yellow eyes. The younger children are quieted, and presently go to sleep. The dirty-legged boy stands for a moment in his shirt, watching the fire. Presently he looks up at her, sees the tears in her eyes, and, throwing his arms round her neck, exclaims: "Mother, I won't never go drovin'; blast me if I do!"

And she hugs him to her worn-out breast and kisses him; and they sit thus together while the sickly daylight breaks over the bush.

F. Scott Fitzgerald to His Daughter

In this letter we see the molding of character: A father gently but explicitly telling his daughter what her duties are.

Dear Pie:

I feel very strongly about your doing duty. Would you give me a little more documentation about your reading in French? I am glad you are happy—but I never believe much in happiness. I never believe in misery either. Those are things you see on the stage or the screen or the printed page, they never really happen to you in life.

All I believe in in life is the rewards for virtue (according to your talents) and the *punishments* for not fulfilling your duties, which are doubly costly. If there is such a volume in the camp library, will you ask Mrs. Tyson to let you look up a sonnet of Shakespeare's in which the line occurs *Lilies that fester smell far worse than weeds.*

Have had no thought today, life seems composed of getting up a *Saturday Evening Post* story. I think of you, and always pleasantly; but if you call me "Pappy" again I'm going to take the White Cat out and beat his bottom *hard, six times for every time you are impertinent.* Do you react to that?

I will arrange the camp bill.

Halfwit, I will conclude. Things to worry about:

Worry about courage

Worry about cleanliness

Worry about efficiency

Worry about horsemanship . . .

Things not to worry about:

Don't worry about popular opinion

Don't worry about dolls

Don't worry about the past

Don't worry about the future

Don't worry about growing up

Don't worry about anybody getting ahead of you

Don't worry about triumph

Don't worry about failure unless it comes through your own fault

Don't worry about mosquitoes

Don't worry about flies

Don't worry about insects in general

Don't worry about parents

Don't worry about boys

Don't worry about disappointments

Don't worry about pleasures

Don't worry about satisfactions . . .

Things to think about:

What am I really aiming at?

How good am I in comparison to my contemporaries in regard to:

(a) Scholarship

(b) Do I really understand about people and am I able to get along with them?

(c) Am I trying to make my body a useful instrument or am I neglecting it?

With dearest love

A Father's Return

AFRICAN FOLKTALE

This wonderful story is told in many different versions in African folklore. This one reminds us that the essence of home and family is one soul reaching for another. And it reminds us that the need of a son for his father ought to be one of the strongest ties that bind a family.

There once was a man who considered himself the happiest man alive because he had a loving wife and four healthy sons. The oldest son was named Keen-Eyes because he could follow tracks through field and jungle better than anyone else in the village. The second son was known as Sharp-Ears because he knew best the call of every creature in the wilderness. The third son was named Strong-Arms because he never failed to win any contest of strength. The fourth son was only a baby, but his father was sure the boy would grow up to be as skilled and devoted as his brothers.

One morning, the family woke to discover the father had disappeared. By nightfall he had not returned, and the next morning brought no sign of his whereabouts.

They talked it over and wondered where he might have gone.

"Perhaps he decided to go visit our uncle," said Keen-Eyes, shrugging his shoulders.

"Or maybe he went to the festival in the next village," suggested Sharp-Ears.

"Or he may have gone into the hills, to enjoy the cool mountain breezes," said Strong-Arms.

Their mother remained quiet and shook her head uncertainly. Another day passed, then a week, and still their father did not return. Sometimes his sons wondered out loud where he might have gone, but after a while they did not talk about it any longer. They feared he was dead.

But the youngest son had no such thoughts, and one morning, as he sat on his mother's lap, he opened his mouth and spoke his first words:

"Where is Father? I want to see my father."

His older brothers gazed at him.

"That's right," said Keen-Eyes. "Where is Father?"

"Some harm may have come to him," said Sharp-Ears.

"We really should go look for him," suggested Strong-Arms.

The three older brothers started out at once, following a path deep into the jungle.

"Look, he came this way," pointed Keen-Eyes. "I can see his tracks on the trail." He led his brothers over hills and into valleys, through fields and woods, farther and farther from home. But at last the tracks disappeared, and even Keen-Eyes lost the trail.

"We must give up," he declared.

"Wait!" urged Sharp-Ears. "I hear someone crying out."

He led his brothers even deeper into the wilderness, farther than they had ever ventured before, pausing every now and then to strain for the sound only he could hear.

At last they came up on a river, and beside it lay their father, holding a growling leopard at bay with his spear!

"We must save him!" yelled Strong-Arms, and without waiting for his brothers, he threw himself onto the pouncing beast and crushed it in his mighty grasp.

"You came just in time," gasped their father. "I came into the jungle to hunt but fell and hurt my leg. I could not make it home. I've lived on what food I could find, but my strength was failing, and the leopard had moved in for the kill."

His sons dressed his wounded leg, brought food to build his strength, and carried him home to their village. Everyone listened to the story of how Keen-Eyes, Sharp-Ears, and Strong-Arms had saved their father, and everyone praised their skill and devotion.

But the fame went to the brothers' heads, and they began to argue among themselves about who was the most responsible for their father's rescue.

"If it were not for me, we would never have known which way to look," boasted Keen-Eyes. "I followed his trail deep into the jungle."

"Yes, but you lost it," reminded Sharp-Ears. "I heard him crying out and led us to the river."

"But what good would that have done if I had not been there?" asked Strong-Arms. "I was the one who killed the leopard and saved our father from certain death."

They debated among themselves, and at last asked their father himself to decide who was the most responsible for his return.

He listened to their arguing and then raised his hand for quiet.

"To all three of you I owe my life," he told them, "for you each played a part in my rescue. But if you ask which of my sons did the most to bring me home, I must tell you it is not you, Keen-Eyes, nor you, Sharp-Ears, not even you, Strong-Arms. The one who truly brought me home is here."

He took his youngest son into his arms.

Then everyone recalled that this was the son whose first words had been, "Where is Father?" It was the little boy's loving heart that had brought his father home.

Four Daughters

SOUTH AMERICAN TALE

This story from South America reminds us that the habits we learn in the home are the habits we carry with us into the world.

There once lived a mother who had four daughters, named Margarita, Emilia, Carmen, and Maria. The three eldest children were lazy and rude and rarely obeyed their mother. Only the youngest, Maria, did what she could to be a loving daughter.

The time came when the mother called her children together.

"You are growing older now, and so am I," she told them. "I will not be able to take care of you forever. You must learn to work so you can make your own ways in the world someday. So I have chores for each of you to do. Margarita, you must dust away the cobwebs. Emilia, you must sweep the floor. Carmen, you must rake the yard. And Maria, you must weed in the garden."

But Margarita, the eldest daughter, scowled.

"Dust? I can't be expected to dust!" she hooted. "I need my beauty sleep." She packed her bag and left the house to find some quiet place to lay down her head.

Emilia, the next daughter, threw up her arms and paced the room in circles.

"I don't know how to sweep," she grunted. "I'm sure I can't learn how. I'm going for a stroll in the countryside. It's much more pleasant there."

She packed her bags and left the house.

Carmen, the next daughter, banged her fist on the table.

"I don't know how to work either!" she shrieked. "I've got better things to do, you know. I'm moving to town. People there know how to have fun."

She, too, packed her bags and left the house with a frown.

Only Maria, the youngest daughter, put on a smile.

"Don't worry, Mother," she said. "I'll work in the garden and plant as many flowers as it will hold, and sell them in town at market. That way I can stay with you and take care of you as you grow old."

Time passed, and Maria kept her word. Her garden flourished, as did her trade at the marketplace, and she made enough money to give some comfort to her mother.

But at last the day came when the old woman sensed her time had come. She sent Maria to find her sisters so she might tell them good-bye.

Maria found Margarita asleep in the shady forest.

"Mother is ill and asks you to come home," she told her.

"I'm sleeping right now," Margarita yawned. "It's much too early. Tell her I'll come later."

Maria found Emilia wandering the countryside, searching the fields for scraps of food left from the harvest.

"I don't have time to come home," she said. "I'm hoping to pick up some dinner."

Maria found Carmen walking the town lanes and alleys, knocking on door after door, looking for handouts.

"I can't come home just now," she muttered. "No one feels generous today. I must keep knocking if I am to eat." She turned her back to rap on another door.

Maria returned to her mother, who grieved at her daughters' fates.

"My Margarita will live in the darkness of the forest for the rest of her life, sleeping the days away," she cried. "My Emilia will spend her life wandering aimlessly, content to live on what lies on the ground. My Carmen will knock and knock for the rest of her days, grubbing for morsels. Only you, Maria, will be welcomed and beloved by all."

The old woman closed her eyes and drew her last breath.

And her prophecy came true.

After her death, Margarita became an owl, and to this day she dwells in the darkest parts of the forest, sleeping the days away.

Emilia turned into a ugly vulture, and now circles the country skies, hoping to dine on whatever she finds lying on the ground.

Carmen changed into a woodpecker, and you can still hear her knocking and knocking all day long, grubbing for morsels.

As for little Maria, she is still hard at work in her garden, tending her flowers, sipping the nectar from their silky cups. And everywhere she goes, she is welcomed and beloved, for Maria turned into a hummingbird.

The Garden of the Frost Flowers

RETOLD BY FRANCES JENKINS OLCOTT

Home is a place of protection from very real dangers beyond the doorstep—dangers from nature and dangers from man. This sad story in which a child dies, retold from a poem by William Cullen Bryant, reminds children that when they are young, they must not stray too far alone, and they must take seriously their parents' warnings.

The Promise Made

In the olden time, long, long ago, there dwelt on a mountainside a cottager, his wife, and his little girl named Eva. A lovely spot was their home, for near it was a glen through which dashed a brook fringed with many sweet-smelling Spring flowers.

But then Winter came, and the little brook was fringed with other blossoms. Strange white ones with crystal leaves and stems grew there in the clear November nights. For when the Winter Winds blew hard, down from the mountaintop came a troop of Little People of the Snow. A beautiful Fairy race they were, with bright locks, and voices like the sounds of steps on crisp Snow. With trailing robes they came, some flying through the air, others tripping lightly across the icy fields.

They threw spangles of silvery Frost upon the grass and edged the brook with glistening parapets. They built crystal bridges over the stream, and, touching the water, turned its face to glass. Then they shook, from their full laps, so many Snowflakes that they covered the whole world with a soft blanket.

Now Eva had often heard about these Little People, but she had never seen them. One Mid-Winter day, when she was twelve years old, she dressed herself warmly to play in the Snow.

"Do not stay too long," said her mother, as she wrapped her furry coat around the child and put on her fur boots. "Do not stay too long, for sharp is the Winter Wind. And go no farther than the great Linden Tree on the edge of our field."

All this Eva promised, and went skipping from the house. Now she climbed the rounded snow swells that felt firm with Frost beneath her feet, and now she slid down them into the deep hollows. So she played alone and was happy.

But as she was clambering up a very high drift, she saw a tiny maiden sitting on the Snow. Lily-cheeked she was, with flowing flaxen hair and blue eyes that gleamed like Ice, while her robe seemed of a more shadowy whiteness than her cheeks.

When she saw Eva, this tiny creature bounded to her feet, and cried: "Oh, come with me, pretty Friend. I have watched you often, and know how well you love the Snow, and how you carve huge-limbed Snowmen, Lions, and Griffins. Come, let us ramble over these bright fields. You shall see what you have never seen before."

So Eva followed her new friend. Together they slid down drifts and climbed white mounds, until they reached the spot where the great Linden Tree stood.

"Here I must stop," said Eva, "for I promised my mother I would go no farther."

But the little Snow Maiden laughed.

"What!" cried she. "Are you afraid of the Snow? Of the pure Snow? Of the innocent Snow? It has never hurt any living thing. Surely your mother made you promise that because she thought you had no one to guide you. I will show you the way and bring you safely home."

By such smooth words Eva was won to break her promise, and she followed her new playmate. Over glistening fields they ran, and down a steep bank to the foot of a huge Snowdrift or Hill of Snow. There the Winds had carved a shelf of driven snow, that curtained a wide opening in the hill.

"Look! Look! Let us enter here!" cried the little creature merrily. "Come, Eva, follow me."

In the Garden of Frost Flowers

Straight under the shelflike curtain Eva and the little Snow Maiden crept, and walked along a passage with white walls. Above them in the vaulted roof were set Snow Stars that cast a wintry twilight over all.

Eva moved with awe and could not speak for wonder; but the little Snow Maiden, laughing gayly, tripped lightly on before. Deeper and deeper they went into the heart of the Hill of Snow. And now the walls began to widen; and the vaulted roof rose higher and higher, until it expanded into a great white dome above their heads.

Eva looked about her. She stood in a large white garden, where everything seemed to be spun out of delicate silent Frost.

At her feet grew snow-white plants with lacelike leaves and spangled flowers. At her side Palm Trees reared their stately white columns tufted with frosted plumes. Huge Oaks, with icelike trunks, waved their transparent branches in the silent air, while their gnarled roots seemed anchored deep in glistening banks. Light sprays of Myrtle, and snowy Roses in bud and bloom, drooped by the winding walks.

All these things—flowers, leaves, and trees—seemed delicately wrought from stainless alabaster. Up the trees ran Jasmine vines with stalks and leaves as colorless as their blossoms. All this Eva saw with wonder and delight.

"Walk, softly, dear Friend," said the little Snow Maiden. "Do not touch the frail creation 'round you, nor sweep it with your skirt.

"Now, look up, and behold how beautifully this Garden of Frost Flowers is lighted. See those shifting gleams that seem to come and go so gently. They are the Northern Lights that make beautiful our Winter Palace.

"Here on long cold nights I and my comrades, the Little People of the Snow, make this garden lovely. We guide to this place the wandering Snowflakes and, piling them up into many quaint shapes, bid them grow into stately columns, glittering arches, white trees, and lovely flowers of Frost.

"But come now, dear Eva, and I will show you a far more wonderful sight."

The Dance of the Little People of the Snow

As she spoke, the little Snow Maiden led her to a window-pane of transparent ice set in the Snow wall.

"Look," said she, "but you may not enter in."

Eva looked.

Lo! She saw a glorious, glistening palace hall from whose lofty roof fell stripes of shimmering light, rose-colored, and delicate green, and tender blue.

This light flowed downward to the floor, enveloping in its rainbow hues a joyous multitude of tiny folk, whirling in a merry dance. Silvery music sounded from cymbals of transparent Ice skillfully touched by tiny hands.

'Round and 'round they flew beneath the dome of colored lights, now wheeling and now turning. Their bright eyes shone under their lily brows. Their gauzy scarfs, sparkling like snow wreaths in the Sun, floated in the dizzy whirl.

Eva stood entranced in wonder, as all these Little People of the Snow, dancing and whirling in the colored lights, swept past the icy windowpane.

Long she gazed, and long she listened to the sweet sounds that thrilled the frosty air. Then the intense cold around her numbed her limbs, and she remembered the promise to her mother.

The Promise Broken

"Alas!" she cried, "too long, too long am I lingering here! Oh, how wickedly I have done to break my promise! What must they think, the dear ones at home?"

With hurried step she found the snowy passage again, and followed it upward to the light, while the little Snow Maiden ran by her side, guiding her feet.

When she reached the open air once more, a bitter blast came rushing from the clear North, chilling her blood, and she shrank in terror before it. But the little Snow Maiden, when she felt the cutting blast, bounded along, uttering shouts of joy, and skipping from drift to drift. And she danced around Eva, as the poor child wearily climbed the slippery mounds of frozen snow.

"Ah me!" sighed Eva at last, "Ah me! My eyes grow heavy. They swim with sleep."

As she spoke, her lids closed, and she sank upon the ground and slept.

Then near her side sat the little Snow Maiden, watching her slumber. She saw the rosy color fade from Eva's rounded cheeks, and the child's brow grow white as marble, while her breath slowly ceased to come and go. All motionless lay her form; and the little Snow Maiden strove to waken her, plucking her dress, and shouting in her ears, but all in vain.

Then suddenly was heard the sound of steps grating on the Snow. It was Eva's parents searching for their lost child. When they found her, lying like a fair marble image in her deathlike sleep, and when they heard from the little Snow Maiden how she had led Eva into the Garden of Frost Flowers, their hearts were wrung with anguish.

They lifted the dear child up and bore her home. And though they chafed her limbs and bathed her brow, she never woke again. The little maid was dead.

Now came the funeral day. In a grave dug in the glen's white side they buried Eva, while from the rocks and hills around a thousand slender voices rose, and sighed, and mourned, until the echoes, taking up the strains, flung them far and wide across the icy fields.

From that day the Little People of the Snow were never seen again. But all during the long, cold Winter nights, invisible tiny hands wove around Eva's grave frost wreaths, and tufts of silvery rime shaped like flowers one scatters on a bier.

The Golden Windows

RETOLD BY LAURA E. RICHARDS

We often dream of the splendors of faraway places, but on inspection those attractions are seldom as precious as home.

All day long the little boy worked hard, in field and barn and shed, for his people were poor farmers, and could not pay a workman; but at sunset there came an hour that was all his own, for his father had given it to him. Then the boy would go up to the top of a hill and look across at another hill that rose some miles away. On this far hill stood a house with windows of clear gold and diamonds. They shone and blazed so that it made the boy wink to look at them. But after a while the people in the house put up shutters, as it seemed, and then it looked like any common farmhouse. The boy supposed they did this because it was suppertime; and then he would go into the house and have his supper of bread and milk, and so to bed.

One day the boy's father called him and said: "You have been a good boy, and have earned a holiday. Take this day for your own; but remember that God gave it, and try to learn some good thing."

The boy thanked his father and kissed his mother. Then he put a piece of bread in his pocket, and started off to find the house with the golden windows.

It was pleasant walking. His bare feet made marks in the white dust, and when he looked back, the footprints seemed to be following him, and making company for him. His shadow, too, kept beside him, and would dance or run with him as he pleased; so it was very cheerful.

By and by he felt hungry, and he sat down by a brown brook that ran through the alder hedge by the roadside, and ate his bread, and drank the clear water. Then he scattered the crumbs for the birds, as his mother had taught him to do, and went on his way.

After a long time he came to a high green hill; and when he had climbed the hill, there was the house on the top. But it seemed that the shutters were up, for he could not see the golden windows. He came up to the house, and then he could well have wept, for the windows were of clear glass, like any others, and there was no gold anywhere about them.

A woman came to the door, and looked kindly at the boy, and asked him what he wanted.

"I saw the golden windows from our hilltop," he said, "and I came to see them, but now they are only glass."

The woman shook her head and laughed.

"We are poor farming people," she said, "and are not likely to have gold about our windows. But glass is better to see through."

She bade the boy sit down on the broad stone step at the door, and brought him a cup of milk and a cake, and bade him rest. Then she called her daughter, a child of his own age, and nodded kindly at the two, and went back to her work.

The little girl was barefooted like himself, and wore a brown cotton gown, but her hair was golden like the windows he had seen, and her eyes were blue like the sky at noon. She led the boy about the farm, and showed him her black calf with the white star on its forehead, and he told her about his own at home, which was red like a chestnut, with four white feet. Then when they had eaten an apple together, and so had become friends, the boy asked her about the golden windows. The little girl nodded, and said she knew all about them, only he had mistaken the house.

"You have come quite the wrong way!" she said. "Come with me, and I will show you the house with the golden windows, and then you will see for yourself."

They went to a knoll that rose behind the farmhouse, and as they went the little girl told him that the golden windows could only be seen at a certain hour, about sunset.

"Yes, I know that!" said the boy.

When they reached the top of the knoll, the girl turned and pointed; and there on a hill far away stood a house with windows of clear gold and diamonds, just as he had seen them. And when they looked again, the boy saw that it was his own home.

Then he told the little girl that he must go. He gave her his best pebble, the white one with the red band, that he had carried for a year in his pocket; and she gave him three horse chestnuts, one red like satin, one spotted, and one white like milk. He kissed her, and promised to come again, but he did not tell her what he had learned. He went back down the hill, and the little girl stood in the sunset light and watched him.

The way home was long, and it was dark before the boy reached his father's house; but the lamplight and firelight shone through the windows, making them almost as bright as he had seen them from the hilltop. When he opened the door, his mother came to kiss him, and his little sister ran to throw her arms about his neck, and his father looked up and smiled from his seat by the fire.

"Have you had a good day?" asked his mother.

Yes, the boy had had a very good day.

"And have you learned anything?" asked his father.

"Yes!" said the boy. "I have learned that our house has windows of gold and diamonds."

The Hampshire Hills

EUGENE FIELD

As this beautiful story reminds us, we go into the world wisely, go through the world bravely, and go out of the world peacefully when we start with the great fortification that is home.

One afternoon many years ago two little brothers named Seth and Abner were playing in the orchard. They were not troubled with the heat of the August day, for a soft, cool wind came up from the river in the valley over yonder and fanned their red cheeks and played all kinds of pranks with their tangled curls. All about them was the hum of bees, the song of birds, the smell of clover, and the merry music of the crickets. Their little dog Fido chased them through the high, waving grass, and rolled with them under the trees, and barked himself hoarse in his attempt to keep pace with their laughter. Wearied at length, they lay beneath the bellflower tree and looked off at the Hampshire hills, and wondered if the time ever would come when they should go out into the world beyond those hills and be great, noisy men. Fido did not understand it at all. He lolled in the grass, cooling his tongue on the clover bloom, and puzzling his brain to know why his little masters were so quiet all at once.

"I wish I were a man," said Abner, ruefully. "I want to be somebody and do something. It is very hard to be a little boy so long and to have no companions but little boys and girls, to see nothing but these same old trees and this same high grass, and to hear nothing but the same bird songs from one day to another."

"That is true," said Seth. "I, too, am very tired of being a little boy, and I long to go out into the world and be a man like my gran'pa or my father or my uncles. With nothing to look at but those distant hills and the river in the valley, my eyes are wearied; and I shall be very happy when I am big enough to leave this stupid place."

Had Fido understood their words he would have chided them, for the little dog loved his home and had no thought of any other pleasure than romping through the orchard and playing with his little masters all the day. But Fido did not understand them.

The clover bloom heard them with sadness. Had they but listened in turn they would have heard the clover saying softly: "Stay with me while you may, little boys; trample me with your merry feet; let me feel the imprint of your curly heads and kiss the sunburn on your little cheeks. Love me while you may, for when you go away you never will come back."

The bellflower tree heard them, too, and she waved her great, strong branches as if she would caress the impatient little lads, and she whispered: "Do not think of leaving me: You are children, and you know nothing of the world beyond those distant hills. It is full of trouble and care and sorrow; abide here in this quiet spot till you are prepared to meet the vexations of that outer world. We are for *you*—we trees and grass and birds and bees and flowers. Abide with us, and learn the wisdom we teach."

The cricket in the raspberry hedge heard them, and she chirped, oh! so sadly: "You will go out into the world and leave us and never think of us again till it is too late to return. Open your ears, little boys, and hear my song of contentment."

So spake the clover bloom and the bellflower tree and the cricket; and in like manner the robin that nested in the linden over yonder, and the big bumblebee that lived in the hole under the pasture gate, and the butterfly and the wild rose pleaded with them, each in his own way; but the little boys did not heed them, so eager were their desires to go into and mingle with the great world beyond those distant hills.

Many years went by; and at last Seth and Abner grew to manhood, and the time was come when they were to go into the world and be brave, strong men. Fido had been dead a long time. They had made him a grave under the bellflower tree— yes, just where he had romped with the two little boys that August afternoon Fido lay sleeping amid the humming of the bees and the perfume of the clover. But Seth and Abner did not think of Fido now, nor did they give even a passing thought to any of their old friends—the bellflower tree, the clover, the cricket, and the robin. Their hearts beat with exultation. They were men, and they were going beyond the hills to know and try the world.

They were equipped for that struggle, not in a vain, frivolous way, but as good and brave young men should be. A gentle mother had counseled them, a prudent father had advised them, and they had gathered from the sweet things of Nature much of that wisdom before which all knowledge is as nothing. So they were fortified. They went beyond the hills and came into the West. How great and busy was the world—how great and busy it was here in the West! What a rush and noise and turmoil and seething and surging, and how keenly did the brothers have to watch and struggle for vantage ground. Withal, they prospered; the counsel of the mother, the advice of the father, the wisdom of the grass and flowers and trees, were much to them, and they prospered. Honor and riches came to them, and they were happy. But amid it all, how seldom they thought of the little home among the circling hills where they had learned the first sweet lessons of life!

And now they were old and gray. They lived in splendid mansions, and all people paid them honor.

One August day a grim messenger stood in Seth's presence and beckoned to him.

"Who are you?" cried Seth. "What strange power have you over me that the very sight of you chills my blood and stays the beating of my heart?"

Then the messenger threw aside his mask, and Seth saw that he was Death. Seth made no outcry; he knew what the summons meant, and he was content. But he sent for Abner.

And when Abner came, Seth was stretched upon his bed, and there was a strange look in his eyes and a flush upon his cheeks, as though a fatal fever had laid hold on him.

"You shall not die!" cried Abner, and he threw himself about his brother's neck and wept.

But Seth bade Abner cease his outcry. "Sit here by my bed-side and talk with me," said he, "and let us speak of the Hampshire hills." A great wonder overcame Abner. With reverence he listened, and as he listened a sweet peace seemed to steal into his soul.

"I am prepared for Death," said Seth, "and I will go with Death this day. Let us talk of our childhood now, for, after all the battle with this great world, it is pleasant to think and speak of our boyhood among the Hampshire hills."

"Say on, dear brother," said Abner.

"I am thinking of an August day long ago," said Seth, solemnly and softly. "It was so *very* long ago, and yet it seems only yesterday. We were in the orchard together, under the bell-flower tree, and our little dog—"

"Fido," said Abner, remembering it all, as the years came back.

"Fido and you and I, under the bellflower tree," said Seth. "How we had played, and how weary we were, and how cool the grass was, and how sweet was the fragrance of the flowers! Can you remember it, brother?"

"Oh, yes," replied Abner, "and I remember how we lay among the clover and looked off at the distant hills and wondered of the world beyond."

"And amid our wonderings and longings," said Seth, "how the old bellflower tree seemed to stretch her kind arms down to us as if she would hold us away from that world beyond the hills."

"And now I can remember that the clover whispered to us,

and the cricket in the raspberry hedge sang to us of content-ment," said Abner.

"The robin, too, caroled in the linden."

"It is very sweet to remember it now," said Seth. "How blue and hazy the hills looked; how cool the breeze blew up from the river; how like a silver lake the old pickerel pond sweltered under the summer sun over beyond the pasture and broom-corn, and how merry was the music of the birds and bees!"

So these old men, who had been little boys together, talked of the August afternoon when with Fido they had romped in the orchard and rested beneath the bellflower tree. And Seth's voice grew fainter, and his eyes were, oh! so dim; but to the very last he spoke of the dear old days and the orchard and the clover and the Hampshire hills. And when Seth fell asleep forever, Abner kissed his brother's lips and knelt at the bedside and said the prayer his mother had taught him.

In the street without there was the noise of passing carts, the cries of tradespeople, and all the bustle of a great and busy city; but, looking upon Seth's dear, dead face, Abner could hear only the music voices of birds and crickets and summer winds as he had heard them with Seth when they were little boys together, back among the Hampshire hills.

The Hiltons' Holiday

SARAH ORNE JEWETT

This story is about the most fundamental of parental responsibilities: spending time with children. Here we find two parents doing their best to instruct their daughters in matters of right conduct. We find the teaching through example of civility, politeness, remembrance of old friends, and thoughtfulness for loved ones. And we discover that in the observance of these daily duties, we win happiness. According to Willa Cather, this was Sarah Orne Jewett's (1849–1909) favorite story.

I

There was a bright, full moon in the clear sky, and the sunset was still shining faintly in the west. Dark woods stood all about the old Hilton farmhouse, save down the hill, westward, where lay the shadowy fields which John Hilton, and his father before him, had cleared and tilled with much toil—the small fields to which they had given the industry and even affection of their honest lives.

John Hilton was sitting on the doorstep of his house. As he

moved his head in and out of the shadows, turning now and then to speak to his wife, who sat just within the doorway, one could see his good face, rough and somewhat unkempt, as if he were indeed a creature of the shady woods and brown earth, instead of the noisy town. It was late in the long spring evening, and he had just come from the lower field as cheerful as a boy, proud of having finished the planting of his potatoes.

"I had to do my last row mostly by feelin'," he said to his wife. "I'm proper glad I pushed through, an' went back an' ended off after supper. 'Twould have taken me a good part o' tomorrow mornin', an' broke my day."

"'Tain't no use for ye to work yourself all to pieces, John," answered the woman quickly. "I declare it does seem harder than ever that we couldn't have kep' our boy; he'd been comin' fourteen years old this fall, most a grown man, and he'd work right 'longside of ye now the whole time."

"'Twas hard to lose him; I do seem to miss little John," said the father sadly. "I expect there was reasons why 'twas best. I feel able an' smart to work; my father was a girt strong man, an' a monstrous worker afore me. 'Tain't that; but I was thinkin' by myself today what a sight o' company the boy would ha' been. You know, small's he was, how I could trust to leave him any-wheres with the team, and how he'd beseech to go with me wherever I was goin'; always right in my tracks I used to tell 'em. Poor little John, for all he was so young he had a great deal o' judgment; he'd ha' made a likely man."

The mother sighed heavily as she sat within the shadow.

"But then there's the little girls, a sight o' help an' company," urged the father eagerly, as if it were wrong to dwell upon sorrow and loss. "Katy, she's most as good as a boy, except that she ain't very rugged. She's a real little farmer, she's helped me a sight this spring; an' you've got Susan Ellen, that makes a complete little housekeeper for ye as far as she's learnt. I don't see but we're better off than most folks, each one us having a workmate."

"That's so, John," acknowledged Mrs. Hilton wistfully, beginning to rock steadily in her straight, splint-bottomed chair. It was always a good sign when she rocked.

"Where be the little girls so late?" asked their father. "'Tis gettin' long past eight o'clock. I don't know when we've all set up so late, but it's so kind o' summerlike an' pleasant. Why, where be they gone?"

"I've told ye; only over to Becker's folks," answered the mother. "I don't see myself what keeps 'em so late; they beseeched me after supper till I let 'em go. They're all in a dazzle with the new teacher; she asked 'em to come over. They say she's unusual smart with 'rethmetic, but she has a kind of a gorpen look to me. She's goin' to give Katy some pieces for her doll, but I told Katy she ought to be ashamed wantin' dolls' pieces, big as she's gettin' to be. I don't know's she ought, though; she ain't but nine this summer."

"Let her take her comfort," said the kindhearted man. "Them things draws her to the teacher, an' makes them acquainted. Katy's shy with new folks, more so'n Susan Ellen, who's of the business kind. Katy's shy-feelin' and wishful."

"I don't know but she is," agreed the mother slowly. "Ain't it sing'lar how well acquainted you be with that one, an' I with Susan Ellen? 'Twas always so from the first. I'm doubtful sometimes our Katy ain't one that'll be like to get married—anyways not about here. She lives right with herself, but Susan Ellen ain't nothin' when she's alone, she's always after company; all the boys is waitin' on her a'ready. I ain't afraid but she'll take her pick when the time comes. I expect to see Susan Ellen well settled—she feels grown up now—but Katy don't care one mite 'bout none o' them things. She wants to be rovin' out-o'-doors. I do believe she'd stand an' hark to a bird the whole forenoon."

"Perhaps she'll grow up to be a teacher," suggested John Hilton. "She takes to her books more 'n the other one. I should like one of 'em to be a teacher same's my mother was. They're good girls as anybody's got."

"So they be," said the mother, with unusual gentleness, and the creak of her rocking chair was heard, regular as the ticking of a clock. The night breeze stirred in the great woods, and the sound of a brook that went falling down the hillside grew louder and louder. Now and then one could hear the plaintive chirp of a bird. The moon glittered with whiteness like a winter moon, and shone upon the low-roofed house until its small windowpanes gleamed like silver, and one could almost see the colors of a blooming bush of lilac that grew in a sheltered angle by the kitchen door. There was an incessant sound of frogs in the lowlands.

"Be you sound asleep, John?" asked the wife presently.

"I don't know but what I was a'most," said the tired man, starting a little. "I should laugh if I was to fall sound asleep right here on the step; 'tis the bright night, I expect, makes my eyes feel heavy, an' 'tis so peaceful. I was up an' dressed a little past four an' out to work. Well, well!" and he laughed sleepily and rubbed his eyes. "Where's the little girls? I'd better step along an' meet 'em."

"I wouldn't just yet; they'll get home all right, but 'tis late for 'em certain. I don't want 'em keepin' Mis' Becker's folks up neither. There, le's wait a few minutes," urged Mrs. Hilton.

"I've be'n a-thinkin' all day I'd like to give the child'n some kind of a treat," said the father, wide awake now. "I hurried up my work 'cause I had it so in mind. They don't have the opportunities some do, an' I want 'em to know the world, an' not stay right here on the farm like a couple o' bushes."

"They're a sight better off not to be so full o' notions as some is," protested the mother suspiciously.

"Certain," answered the farmer; "but they're good, bright child'n, an' commencin' to take a sight o' notice. I want 'em to have all we can give 'em. I want 'em to see how other folks does things."

"Why, so do I"—here the rocking chair stopped ominously—"but so long's they're contented—"

"Contented ain't all in this world; hopper-toads may have that quality an' spend all their time a-blinkin'. I don't know's bein' contented is all there is to look for in a child. Ambition's somethin' to me."

"Now you've got your mind onto some plot or other." (The rocking chair began to move again.) "Why can't you talk right out?"

"'Tain't nothin' special," answered the good man, a little ruffled; he was never prepared for his wife's mysterious powers of divination. "Well there, you do find things out the master! I only thought perhaps I'd take 'em tomorrow, an' go off somewhere if 'twas a good day. I've been promisin' for a good while I'd take 'em to Topham Corners; they've never been there since they was very small."

"I believe you want a good time yourself. You ain't never got over bein' a boy." Mrs. Hilton seemed much amused. "There, go if you want to an' take 'em; they've got their summer hats an' new dresses. I don't know o' nothin' that stands in the way. I should sense it better if there was a circus or anythin' to go to. Why don't you wait an' let the girls pick 'em some strawberries or nice ros'berries, and then they could take an' sell 'em to the stores?"

John Hilton reflected deeply. "I should like to get me some good yellow-turnip seed to plant late. I ain't more'n satisfied with what I've been gettin' o' late years o' Ira Speed. An' I'm goin' to provide me with a good hoe; mine's gettin' wore out an' all shackly. I can't seem to fix it good."

"Them's excuses," observed Mrs. Hilton, with friendly tolerance. "You just cover up the hoe with somethin', if you get it—I would. Ira Speed's so jealous he'll remember it of you this twenty year, your goin' an' buyin' a new hoe o' anybody but him."

"I've always thought 'twas a free country," said John Hilton soberly. "I don't want to vex Ira neither; he favors us all he can in trade. 'Tis difficult for him to spare a cent, but he's as honest as daylight."

At this moment there was a sudden sound of young voices, and a pair of young figures came out from the shadow of the woods into the moonlighted open space. An old cock crowed loudly from his perch in the shed, as if he were a herald of royalty. The little girls were hand in hand, and a brisk young dog capered about them as they came.

"Wa'n't it dark gittin' home through the woods this time o' night?" asked the mother hastily, and not without reproach.

"I don't love to have you gone so late; Mother an' me was

timid about ye, and you've kep' Mis' Becker's folks up, I expect," said their father regretfully. "I don't want to have it said that my little girls ain't got good manners."

"The teacher had a party," chirped Susan Ellen, the elder of the two children. "Goin' home from school she asked the Grover boys, an' Mary an' Sarah Speed. An' Mis' Becker was real pleasant to us: She passed round some cake, an' handed us sap sugar on one of her best plates, an' we played games an' sung some pieces too. Mis' Becker thought we did real well. I can pick out most of a tune on the cabinet organ; teacher says she'll give me lessons."

"I want to know, dear!" exclaimed John Hilton.

"Yes, an' we played Copenhagen, an' took sides spellin', an' Katy beat everybody spellin' there was there."

Katy had not spoken; she was not so strong as her sister, and while Susan Ellen stood a step or two away addressing her eager little audience, Katy had seated herself close to her father on the doorstep. He put his arm around her shoulders, and drew her close to his side, where she stayed.

"Ain't you got nothin' to tell, daughter?" he asked, looking down fondly; and Katy gave a pleased little sigh for answer.

"Tell 'em what's goin' to be the last day o' school, and about our trimmin' the schoolhouse," she said; and Susan Ellen gave the program in most spirited fashion.

"'Twill be a great time," said the mother, when she had finished. "I don't see why folks wants to go traipsin' off to strange places when such things is happenin' right about 'em." But the children did not observe her mysterious air. "Come, you must step yourselves right to bed!"

They all went into the dark, warm house; the bright moon shone steadily all night, and the lilac flowers were shaken by no breath of wind until the early dawn.

II

The Hiltons always waked early. So did their neighbors, the crows and song sparrows and robins, the light-footed foxes and squirrels in the woods. When John Hilton waked, before five o'clock, an hour later than usual because he had sat up so late, he opened the house door and came out into the yard, crossing the short green turf hurriedly as if the day were too far spent for any loitering. The magnitude of the plan for taking a whole day of pleasure confronted him seriously, but the weather was fair, and his wife, whose disapproval could not have been set aside, had accepted and even smiled upon the great project. It was inevitable now that he and the children should go to Topham Corners. Mrs. Hilton had the pleasure of waking them, and telling the news.

In a few minutes they came frisking out to talk over the great plans. The cattle were already fed, and their father was milking. The only sign of high festivity was the wagon pulled out into the yard, with both seats put in as if it were Sunday; but Mr. Hilton still wore his everyday clothes, and Susan Ellen suffered instantly from disappointment.

"Ain't we goin', Father?" she asked complainingly; but he nodded and smiled at her, even though the cow, impatient to get to pasture, kept whisking her rough tail across his face. He held his head down and spoke cheerfully, in spite of this vexation.

"Yes, sister, we're goin' certain', an' goin' to have a great time, too." Susan Ellen thought that he seemed like a boy at that delightful moment, and felt new sympathy and pleasure at once. "You go an' help Mother about breakfast an' them things; we want to get off quick's we can. You coax Mother now, both on ye, an' see if she won't go with us."

"She said she wouldn't be hired to," responded Susan Ellen. "She says it's goin' to be hot, an' she's laid out to go over an' see how her aunt Tamsen Brooks is this afternoon."

The father gave a little sigh; then he took heart again. The truth was that his wife made light of the contemplated pleasure, and, much as he usually valued her companionship and approval, he was sure that they should have a better time without her. It was impossible, however, not to feel guilty of disloyalty at the thought. Even though she might be completely unconscious of his best ideals, he only loved her and the ideals the more, and bent his energies to satisfying her indefinite expectations. His wife still kept much of that youthful beauty which Susan Ellen seemed likely to reproduce.

An hour later the best wagon was ready, and the great expedition set forth. The little dog sat apart, and barked as if it fell entirely upon him to voice the general excitement. Both seats were in the wagon, but the empty place testified to Mrs. Hilton's unyielding disposition. She had wondered why one broad seat would not do, but John Hilton meekly suggested that the wagon looked better with both. The little girls sat on the backseat dressed alike in their Sunday hats of straw with blue ribbons, and their little plaid shawls pinned neatly about their small shoulders. They wore gray thread gloves, and sat very straight. Susan Ellen was half a head the taller, but otherwise, from behind, they looked much alike. As for their father, he was in his Sunday best—a plain black coat, and a winter hat of felt, which was heavy and rusty-looking for that warm early summer day. He had it in mind to buy a new straw hat at Topham, so that this with the turnip seed and the hoe made three important reasons for going.

"Remember an' lay off your shawls when you get there an' carry them over your arms," said the mother, clucking like an excited hen to her chickens. "They'll do to keep the dust off your new dresses goin' an' comin'. An' when you eat your dinners don't get spots on you, an' don't point at folks as you ride by, an' stare, or they'll know you come from the country. An', John, you call into Cousin Ad'line Marlow's an' see how they all be, an' tell her I expect her over certain to stop awhile before hayin'. It always eases her phthisic to git up here on the high land. An' don't come home all wore out; an', John, don't you go an' buy me no kickshaws to fetch home. I ain't a child, an' you ain't got no money to waste. I expect you'll go, like's not, an' buy you some kind of a foolish boy's hat; do look an' see if it's reasonable good straw, an' won't splinter all off round the edge. An' you mind, John—"

"Yes, yes, hold on!" cried John impatiently; then he cast a last affectionate, reassuring look at her face, flushed with the hurry and responsibility of starting them off in proper shape. "I wish you was goin', too," he said, smiling. "I do so!" Then the old horse started, and they went out at the bars, and began the careful long descent of the hill. The young dog, tethered to the lilac bush, was frantic with piteous appeals; the little girls piped their eager good-byes again and again, and their father turned many times to look back and wave his hand. As for their mother, she stood alone and watched them out of sight.

There was one place far out on the high road where she could catch a last glimpse of the wagon, and she waited what seemed a very long time until it appeared and then was lost to sight again behind a low hill. "They're nothin' but a pack o' child'n together," she said aloud; and then felt lonelier than she expected. She even stooped and petted the unresigned little dog as she passed him, going into the house.

The occasion was so much more important than anyone had foreseen that both the little girls were speechless. It seemed at first like going to church in new clothes; or to a funeral; they hardly knew how to behave at the beginning of a whole day of pleasure. They made grave bows at such persons of their acquaintance as happened to be straying in the road. Once or twice they stopped before a farmhouse, while their father talked an inconsiderately long time with someone about the crops and the weather, and even dwelt upon town business and the doings of the selectmen, which might be talked of at any time. The explanations that he gave of their excursion seemed quite unnecessary. It was made entirely clear that he had a little business to do at Topham Corners, and thought he had better give the little girls a ride; they had been very steady at school, and he had finished planting, and could take the day as well as not. Soon, however, they all felt as if such an excursion were an everyday affair, and Susan Ellen began to ask eager questions, while Katy silently sat apart, enjoying herself as she never had done before. She liked to see the strange houses, and the children who belonged to them; it was delightful to find flowers that she knew growing all along the road, no matter how far she went from home. Each small homestead looked its best and pleasantest, and shared the exquisite beauty that early summer made—shared the luxury of greenness and floweriness that decked the rural world. There was an early peony or a late lilac in almost every dooryard.

It was seventeen miles to Topham. After a while they seemed very far from home, having left the hills far behind, and descended to a great level country with fewer tracts of woodland, and wider fields where the crops were much more forward. The houses were all painted, and the roads were smoother and wider. It had been so pleasant driving along that Katy dreaded going into the strange town when she first caught sight of it, though Susan Ellen kept asking with bold fretfulness if they were not almost there. They counted the steeples of four churches, and their father presently showed them the Topham Academy, where their grandmother once went to school, and told them that perhaps someday they would go there, too. Katy's heart gave a strange leap; it was such a tremendous thing to think of, but instantly the suggestion was transformed for her into one of the certainties of life. She looked with solemn awe at the tall belfry, and the long rows of windows in the front of the academy, there where it stood high and white among the clustering trees. She hoped that they were going to drive by, but something forbade her taking the responsibility of saying so.

Soon the children found themselves among the crowded village houses. Their father turned to look at them with affectionate solicitude.

"Now sit up straight and appear pretty," he whispered to

them. "We're among the best people now, an' I want folks to
think well of you."

"I guess we're as good as they be," remarked Susan Ellen, looking at some innocent passersby with dark suspicion, but Katy
tried indeed to sit straight, and folded her hands prettily in her
lap, and wished with all her heart to be pleasing for her father's
sake. Just then an elderly woman saw the wagon and the sedate
party it carried, and smiled so kindly that it seemed to Katy as if
Topham Corners had welcomed and received them. She smiled
back again as if this hospitable person were an old friend, and
entirely forgot that the eyes of all Topham had been upon her.

"There, now we're coming to an elegant house that I want
you to see; you'll never forget it," said John Hilton. "It's where
Judge Masterson lives, the great lawyer; the handsomest house
in the county, everybody says."

"Do you know him, Father?" asked Susan Ellen.

"I do," answered John Hilton proudly. "Him and my mother
went to school together in their young days, and were always
called the two best scholars of their time. The judge called to see
her once; he stopped to our house to see her when I was a boy.
An' then, some years ago—you've heard me tell how I was on
the jury, an' when he heard my name spoken he looked at me
sharp, and asked if I wa'n't the son of Catharine Winn, an'
spoke most beautiful of your grandmother, an' how well I
remembered their young days together."

"I like to hear about that," said Katy.

"She had it pretty hard, I'm afraid, up on the old farm. She
keepin' school in our district when Father married her—that's
the main reason I backed 'em down when they wanted to tear

the old schoolhouse all to pieces," confided John Hilton, turning eagerly. "They all say she lived longer up here on the hill than she could anywhere, but she never had her health. I wa'n't but a boy when she died. Father an' me lived alone afterward till the time your mother come; 'twas a good while, too; I wa'n't married so young as some. 'Twas lonesome, I tell you; Father was plumb discouraged losin' of his wife, an' her long sickness an' all set him back, an' we'd work all day on the land an' never say a word. I s'pose 'tis bein' so lonesome early in life that makes me so pleased to have some nice girls growin' up round me now."

There was a tone in her father's voice that drew Katy's heart toward him with new affection. She dimly understood, but Susan Ellen was less interested. They had often heard this story before, but to one child it was always new and to the other old. Susan Ellen was apt to think it tiresome to hear about her grandmother, who, being dead, was hardly worth talking about.

"There's Judge Masterson's place," said their father in an everyday manner, as they turned a corner, and came into full view of the beautiful old white house standing behind its green trees and terraces and lawns. The children had never imagined anything so stately and fine, and even Susan Ellen exclaimed with pleasure. At that moment they saw an old gentleman, who carried himself with great dignity, coming slowly down the wide box-bordered path toward the gate.

"There he is now, there's the judge!" whispered John Hilton excitedly, reining his horse quickly to the green roadside. "He's goin' downtown to his office; we can wait right here an' see him. I can't expect him to remember me; it's been a good many years. Now you are goin' to see the great Judge Masterson!"

There was a quiver of expectation in their hearts. The judge stopped at his gate, hesitating a moment before he lifted the latch, and glanced up the street at the country wagon with its two prim little girls on the backseat, and the eager man who drove. They seemed to be waiting for something; the old horse was nibbling at the fresh roadside grass. The judge was used to being looked at with interest, and responded now with a smile as he came out to the sidewalk, and unexpectedly turned their way. Then he suddenly lifted his hat with grave politeness, and came directly toward them.

"Good morning, Mr. Hilton," he said. "I am very glad to see you, sir"; and Mr. Hilton, the little girls' own father, took off his hat with equal courtesy, and bent forward to shake hands.

Susan Ellen cowered and wished herself away, but little Katy sat straighter than ever, with joy in her father's pride and pleasure shining in her pale, flowerlike little face.

"These are your daughters, I am sure," said the old gentleman kindly, taking Susan Ellen's limp and reluctant hand; but when he looked at Katy, his face brightened. "How she recalls your mother!" he said with great feeling. "I am glad to see this dear child. You must come to see me with your father, my dear," he added, still looking at her. "Bring both the little girls, and let them run about the old garden; the cherries are just getting ripe," said Judge Masterson hospitably. "Perhaps you will have time to stop this afternoon as you go home?"

"I should call it a great pleasure if you would come and see us again some time. You may be driving our way, sir," said John Hilton.

"Not very often in these days," answered the old judge. "I

thank you for the kind invitation. I should like to see the fine view again from your hill westward. Can I serve you in any way while you are in town? Good-bye, my little friends!"

Then they parted, but not before Katy, the shy Katy, whose hand the judge still held unconsciously while he spoke, had reached forward as he said good-bye, and lifted her face to kiss him. She could not have told why, except that she felt drawn to something in the serious, worn face. For the first time in her life the child had felt the charm of manners; perhaps she owned a kinship between that which made him what he was, and the spark of nobleness and purity in her own simple soul. She turned again and again to look back at him as they drove away.

"Now you have seen one of the first gentlemen in the county," said their father. "It was worth comin' twice as far"— but he did not say any more, nor turn as usual to look in the children's faces.

In the chief business street of Topham a great many country wagons like the Hiltons' were fastened to the posts, and there seemed to our holidaymakers to be a great deal of noise and excitement.

"Now I've got to do my errands, and we can let the horse rest and feed," said John Hilton. "I'll slip his headstall right off, an' put on his halter. I'm goin' to buy him a real good treat o' oats. First we'll go an' buy me my straw hat; I feel as if this one looked a little past to wear in Topham. We'll buy the things we want, an' then we'll walk all along the street, so you can look in the windows an' see the han'some things, same's your mother likes to. What was it Mother told you about your shawls?"

"To take 'em off an' carry 'em over our arms," piped Susan

Ellen, without comment, but in the interest of alighting and finding themselves afoot upon the pavement the shawls were forgotten. The children stood at the doorway of a shop while their father went inside, and they tried to see what the Topham shapes of bonnets were like, as their mother had advised them; but everything was exciting and confusing, and they could arrive at no decision. When Mr. Hilton came out with a hat in his hand to be seen in a better light, Katy whispered that she wished he would buy a shiny one like Judge Masterson's; but her father only smiled and shook his head, and said that they were plain folks, he and Katy. There were dry goods for sale in the same shop, and a young clerk who was measuring linen kindly pulled off some pretty labels with gilded edges and gay pictures, and gave them to the little girls, to their exceeding joy. He may have had small sisters at home, this friendly lad, for he took pains to find two pretty blue boxes besides, and was rewarded by their beaming gratitude.

It was a famous day; they even became used to seeing so many people pass. The village was full of its morning activity, and Susan Ellen gained a new respect for her father, and an increased sense of her own consequence, because even in Topham several persons knew him and called him familiarly by name. The meeting with an old man who had once been a neighbor seemed to give Mr. Hilton the greatest pleasure. The old man called to them from a house doorway as they were passing, and they all went in. The children seated themselves wearily on the wooden step, but their father shook his old friend eagerly by the hand, and declared that he was delighted to see him so well and enjoying the fine weather.

"Oh, yes," said the old man, in a feeble, quavering voice. "I'm astonishin' well for my age. I don't complain, John, I don't complain."

They talked long together of people whom they had known in the past, and Katy, being a little tired, was glad to rest, and sat still with her hands folded, looking about the front yard. There were some kinds of flowers that she never had seen before.

"This is the one that looks like my mother," her father said, and touched Katy's shoulder to remind her to stand up and let herself be seen. "Judge Masterson saw the resemblance; we met him at his gate this morning."

"Yes, she certain does look like your mother, John," said the old man, looking pleasantly at Katy, who found that she liked him better than at first. "She does, certain; the best of young folks is, they remind us of the old ones. 'Tis nateral to cling to life, folks say, but for me, I git impatient at times. Most everybody's gone now, an' I want to be goin'. 'Tis somethin' before me, an' I want to have it over with. I want to be there 'long o' the rest o' the folks. I expect to last quite a while, though; I may see ye couple o' times more, John."

John Hilton responded cheerfully, and the children were urged to pick some flowers. The old man awed them with his impatience to be gone. There was such a townful of people about him, and he seemed as lonely as if he were the last survivor of a former world. Until that moment they had felt as if everything were just beginning.

"Now I want to buy somethin' pretty for your mother," said Mr. Hilton, as they went soberly away down the street, the children keeping fast hold of his hands. "By now the old horse will have eat his dinner and had a good rest, so pretty soon we can jog along home. I'm goin' to take you round by the academy, and the old North Meetinghouse where Dr. Barstow used to preach. Can't you think o' somethin' that your mother'd want?" he asked suddenly, confronted by a man's difficulty of choice.

"She was talkin' about wantin' a new pepper box, one day; the top o' the old one won't stay on," suggested Susan Ellen, with delightful readiness. "Can't we have some candy, Father?"

"Yes, ma'am," said John Hilton, smiling and swinging her hand to and fro as they walked. "I feel as if some would be good myself. What's all this?" They were passing a photographer's doorway with its enticing array of portraits. "I do declare!" he exclaimed excitedly, "I'm goin' to have our pictures taken; 'twill please your mother more 'n a little."

This was, perhaps, the greatest triumph of the day, except the delightful meeting with the judge; they sat in a row, with the father in the middle, and there was no doubt as to the excellence of the likeness. The best hats had to be taken off because they cast a shadow, but they were not missed, as their owners had feared. Both Susan Ellen and Katy looked their brightest and best; their eager young faces would forever shine there; the joy of the holiday was mirrored in the little picture. They did not know why their father was so pleased with it; they would not know until age had dowered them with the riches of association and remembrance.

Just at nightfall the Hiltons reached home again, tired out and happy. Katy had climbed over into the front seat beside her father, because that was always her place when they went to church on Sundays. It was a cool evening, there was a fresh sea wind that brought a light mist with it, and the sky was fast growing cloudy. Somehow the children looked different; it seemed to their mother as if they had grown older and taller since they went away in the morning, and as if they belonged to the town now as much as to the country. The greatness of their day's experience had left her far behind; the day had been silent and lonely without them, and she had their supper ready, and been watching anxiously, ever since five o'clock. As for the children themselves they had little to say at first—they had eaten their luncheon early on the way to Topham. Susan Ellen was childishly cross, but Katy was pathetic and wan. They could hardly wait to show the picture, and their mother was as much pleased as everybody had expected.

"There, what did make you wear your shawls?" she exclaimed a moment afterward, reproachfully. "You ain't been an' wore 'em all day long? I wanted folks to see how pretty your new dresses was, if I did make 'em. Well, well! I wish more 'n ever now I'd gone an' seen to ye!"

"An' here's the pepper box!" said Katy, in a pleased, unconscious tone.

"That really is what I call beautiful," said Mrs. Hilton, after a long and doubtful look. "Our other one was only tin. I never did look so high as a chiny one with flowers, but I can get us another anytime for everyday. That's a proper hat, as good as you could have got, John. Where's your new hoe?" she asked as he came toward her from the barn, smiling with satisfaction.

"I declare to Moses if I didn't forget all about it," meekly acknowledged the leader of the great excursion. "That an' my yellow-turnip seed, too; they went clean out o' my head, there was so many other things to think of. But 'tain't no sort o' matter; I can get a hoe just as well to Ira Speed's."

His wife could not help laughing. "You an' the little girls have had a great time. They was full o' wonder to me about everything, and I expect they'll talk about it for a week. I guess we was right about havin' 'em see somethin' more o' the world."

"Yes," answered John Hilton, with humility, "yes, we did have a beautiful day. I didn't expect so much. They looked as nice as anybody, and appeared so modest an' pretty. The little girls will remember it perhaps by an' by. I guess they won't never forget this day they had 'long o' Father."

―――――――

It was evening again, the frogs were piping in the lower meadows, and in the woods, higher up the great hill, a little owl began to hoot. The sea air, salt and heavy, was blowing in our country at the end of the hot bright day. A lamp was lighted in the house, the happy children were talking together, and supper was waiting. The father and mother lingered for a moment outside and looked down over the shadowy fields; then they went in, without speaking. The great day was over, and they shut the door.

Icarus and Daedalus

This famous Greek myth reminds us exactly why young people have a responsibility to obey their parents—for the same good reason parents have a responsibility to guide their children: There are many things adults know that young people do not. The ancient Greek dramatist Aeschylus put it this way: "Obedience is the mother of success and is wedded to safety." Safe childhoods and successful upbringings require a measure of obedience, as Icarus finds out the hard way.

Daedalus was the most skillful builder and inventor of his day in ancient Greece. He built magnificent palaces and gardens, and created wonderful works of art throughout the land. His statues were so beautifully crafted they were taken for living beings, and it was believed they could see and walk about. People said someone as cunning as Daedalus must have learned the secrets of his craft from the gods themselves.

Now across the sea, on the island of Crete, lived a king named Minos. King Minos had a terrible monster that was half bull and half man called the Minotaur, and he needed someplace to keep it. When he heard of Daedalus's cleverness, he invited him to come to his country and build a prison to hold the beast. So Daedalus and his young son, Icarus, sailed to Crete, and there Daedalus built the famous Labyrinth, a maze of winding passages so tangled and twisted that whoever went in could never find the way out. And there they put the Minotaur.

When the Labyrinth was finished, Daedalus wanted to sail back to Greece with his son, but Minos had made up his mind to keep them in Crete. He wanted Daedalus to stay and invent more wonderful devices for him, so he locked them both in a high tower beside the sea. The king knew Daedalus was clever enough to escape from the tower, so he also ordered that every ship be searched for stowaways before sailing from Crete.

Other men may have given up, but not Daedalus. From his high tower he watched the sea gulls drifting on the ocean breezes. "Minos may control the land and the sea," he said, "but he does not rule the air. We'll go that way."

So he summoned all the secrets of his craft, and he set to work. Little by little, he gathered a great pile of feathers of all sizes. He fastened them together with thread, and molded them with wax, and at last he had two great wings like those of the sea gulls. He tied them to his shoulders, and after one or two clumsy efforts, he found that by waving his arms he could rise into the air. He held himself aloft, wavering this way and that with the wind, until he taught himself how to glide and soar on the currents as gracefully as any gull.

Next he built a second pair of wings for Icarus. He taught the boy how to move the feathers and rise a few feet into the air, and then let him fly back and forth across the room. Then he taught him how to ride the air currents, climbing in circles, and hang in the winds. They practiced together until Icarus was ready.

Finally the day came when the winds were just right. Father and son strapped on their wings and prepared to fly home.

"Remember all I've told you," Daedalus said. "Above all, remember you must not fly too high or too low. If you fly too low, the ocean sprays will clog your wings and make them too heavy. If you fly too high, the heat of the sun will melt the wax, and your wings will fall apart. Stay close to me, and you'll be fine."

Up they rose, the boy after his father, and the hateful ground of Crete sank far beneath them. As they flew the plowman stopped his work to gaze, and the shepherd leaned on his staff to watch them, and people came running out of their houses to catch a glimpse of the two figures high above the treetops. Surely they were gods—Apollo, perhaps, with Cupid after him.

At first the flight seemed terrible to both Daedalus and Icarus. The wide, endless sky dazed them, and even the quickest glance down made their brains reel. But gradually they grew used to riding among the clouds, and they lost their fear. Icarus felt the wind fill his wings and lift him higher and higher, and began to sense a freedom he had never known before. He looked down with great excitement at all the islands they passed, and their people, and at the broad blue sea spread out beneath him, dotted with the white sails of ships. He soared higher and higher, forgetting his father's warning. He forgot everything in the world but joy.

"Come back!" Daedalus called frantically. "You're flying too high! Remember the sun! Come down! Come down!"

But Icarus thought of nothing but his own excitement and glory. He longed to fly as close as he could to the heavens. Nearer and nearer he came to the sun, and slowly his wings began to soften. One by one the feathers began to fall and scatter in the air, and suddenly the wax melted all at once. Icarus felt himself falling. He fluttered his arms as fast as he could, but no feathers remained to hold the air. He cried out for his father, but it was too late—with a scream he fell from his lofty height and plunged into the sea, disappearing beneath the waves.

Daedalus circled over the water again and again, but he saw nothing but feathers floating on the waves, and he knew his son was gone. At last the body came to the surface, and he managed to pluck it from the sea. With a heavy burden and broken heart Daedalus slowly flew away. When he reached land, he buried his son and built a temple to the gods. Then he hung up his wings, and never flew again.

The Legend of the Christ Child

ADAPTED FROM A RETELLING
BY ELIZABETH HARRISON

This beautiful old story reminds us that in homes where love is, God is.

O nce upon a time, long, long ago, on the night before Christmas, a little child was wandering all alone through the streets of a great city. There were many people in the street, fathers and mothers, sisters and brothers, uncles and aunts, and even gray-haired grandfathers and grandmothers, all of whom were hurrying home with bundles of presents for each other and for their little ones. Fine carriages rolled by, express wagons rattled past, even old carts were pressed into service. All things seemed in a hurry and glad with expectation of the coming Christmas morning.

From some of the windows bright lights were already beginning to stream, until it was almost as bright as day. But the little child seemed to have no home, and wandered about listlessly from street to street. No one took any notice of him, except perhaps Jack Frost, who bit his bare toes and made the ends of his fingers tingle. The north wind, too, seemed to notice the child, for it blew against him and pierced his ragged garments through and through, causing him to shiver with cold. Home after home he passed, looking with longing eyes through the windows in upon the glad, happy children, most of whom were helping to trim the Christmas trees for the coming morrow.

"Surely," said the child to himself, "where there is so much gladness and happiness, some of it may be for me." So with timid steps he approached a large and handsome house. Through the windows he could see a beautiful Christmas tree already lighted. Many presents hung upon it. Its green boughs were trimmed with gold and silver ornaments. Slowly he climbed up the broad steps and gently rapped at the door.

It was opened by a tall and stately footman. He had a kindly face, although his voice was deep and gruff. He looked at the little child for a moment, then sadly shook his head and said, "Go down off the steps. There is no room here for such as you." He looked sorry as he spoke. Through the open door a bright light shone, and the warm air, filled with the fragrance of the Christmas pine, rushed out from the inner room and greeted the little wanderer like a kiss. As the child turned back into the cold and darkness, he wondered why the footman had spoken thus, for surely, thought he, those little children would love to have another companion join them in their joyous Christmas festival. But the little children inside did not even know that he had knocked at the door.

The street grew colder and darker as the child passed on. He went sadly forward, saying to himself, "Is there no one in all this great city who will share Christmas with me?" Farther and farther down the street he wandered, to where the homes were not so large and beautiful. There seemed to be little children inside of nearly all the houses. They were dancing and frolicking about. Christmas trees could be seen in every window, with beautiful dolls and trumpets and picture books and balls and tops and other wonderful toys hung upon them.

In one window the child noticed a little lamb made of soft, white wool. Around its neck was tied a red ribbon. It had evidently been hung on the tree for one of the younger children. The little wanderer stopped before this window and looked long and earnestly at the beautiful things inside, but most of all was he drawn toward the white lamb.

At last, creeping up to the windowpane, he gently tapped upon it. A little girl came to the window and looked out into the dark street where the snow had now begun to fall. She saw the child, but she only frowned and shook her head, and said, "Go away and come some other time. We are too busy to take care of you now." Back into the dark, cold street he turned again. The wind was whirling past him and seemed to say, "Hurry on, hurry on, we have no time to stop. 'Tis Christmas Eve and everybody is in a hurry tonight."

Again and again the child rapped softly at door or windowpane. At each place he was refused admission. One mother feared he might have some ugly disease which her darlings would catch; another father said he had only enough for his own children, and none to spare for beggar brats. Still another told him to go home where he belonged, and not to trouble other folks.

The hours passed; the night grew later, and the wind colder, and the street darker. Farther and farther the little one wandered. There was scarcely anyone left on the streets by this time, and the few who remained did not notice the child. Suddenly ahead of him there appeared a bright, single ray of light. It shone through the darkness into the child's eyes. He looked up, smiling, and said, "I will go where the little light beckons. Perhaps they will share their Christmas with me."

Hurrying past all the other houses he soon reached the end of the street and went straight up to the window from which the light was streaming. The house was old and small, but the child cared not for that. The light seemed still to call him in. From what do you suppose the light came? Nothing but a candle which had been placed in an old cup with a broken handle, in the window, as a glad token of Christmas Eve. There was neither curtain nor shade at the small, square window, and as the little child looked in he saw standing upon a neat, wooden table a small Christmas tree. The room was plainly furnished, but it was very clean. Near the fireplace sat a sweet-faced mother with a little two-year-old on her knee and an older child beside her. The two children were looking into their mother's face and listening to a story. She must have been telling them a Christmas story, I think. A few bright coals were burning in the fireplace, and all seemed light and warm within.

The little wanderer crept closer to the windowpane. So sweet was the mother's face, so loving seemed the little children, that he took courage and tapped gently, very gently, on the door. The mother stopped talking, the little children looked up. "What was that, Mother?" asked the little girl at her side.

"I think it was someone tapping on the door," replied the mother. "Run quickly and open it, dear, for it is a bitter cold night to keep anyone waiting in this storm."

"Oh, Mother, I think it was the bough of the tree tapping against the windowpane," said the little girl. "Do please go on with our story."

Again the little wanderer tapped upon the door.

"My child! My child!" exclaimed the mother, rising. "That certainly was a rap on the door. Run quickly and open it. No one must be left out in the cold on Christmas Eve."

The child ran to the door and threw it wide open. The mother saw the ragged stranger standing without, cold and shivering, with bare head and almost bare feet. She held out both hands and drew him into the warm, bright room. "You poor dear child," was all she said, and, putting her arms around him, she drew him close to her breast. "He is very cold, my children," she exclaimed. "We must warm him."

"And," added the little girl, "we must love him and give him some of our Christmas, too."

"Yes," said the mother, "but first let us warm him."

The mother sat down beside the fire with the child on her lap, and her own two little ones warmed his half-frozen hands in theirs. The mother smoothed his tangled curls, and, bending low over his head, kissed the child's forehead. She gathered the three little ones close to her and the candle and the firelight shone over them. For a moment the room was very still. I think she must have been praying. Then she whispered to the little girl, who ran into the other room and returned with a bowl of bread and milk for the little stranger.

By and by the little girl said, softly, to her mother, "May we not light the Christmas tree, and let him see how beautiful it looks?"

"Yes," replied the mother. With that she seated the child on a low stool beside the fire, and went herself to fetch the few simple ornaments which from year to year she had saved for her children's Christmas tree.

And as they busied themselves about the tree, they began to notice that the room had filled with a strange and wonderful light. Brighter and brighter it grew, until it shone like the sun; from floor to ceiling all was light as day. And when they turned and looked at the spot where the little wanderer had sat, it was empty. There was nothing to be seen. The child was gone, but the light was still in the room.

"Children," the mother said quietly, "I believe we have had the Christ Child with us tonight."

And she drew her dear ones to her and kissed them, and there was great joy in the little house.

The Matsuyama Mirror

JAPANESE FOLKTALE

This charming Japanese tale was popular with American children around the turn of the twentieth century. It was handed down from parent to child in Japan over many generations and dates to a time when people living outside of cities knew nothing of mirrors or their uses. It reminds us that in many ways, we grow up in our parents' image. We hope their virtues become our virtues.

I

Long ago there lived, in a quiet spot in faraway Japan, a young man and his wife. They had one child, a little daughter, whom they loved dearly. I cannot tell you their names, for they have been long since forgotten; but the name of the place where they lived was Matsuyama.

It happened once, while the little girl was still a baby, that the father had to go to the great city, the capital of Japan, upon some business. It was too far for the mother and her little baby to go, so he set out alone, after bidding them good-bye and promising to bring them home some pretty present.

The mother had never been farther from home than the next village, and she could not help being a little frightened at the thought of her husband taking such a long journey; and yet she was a little proud, too, for he was the first man in all that countryside who had been to the big town where the King and his great lords lived, and where there were so many beautiful and curious things to be seen.

At last the time came when she might expect her husband back, so she dressed the baby in her best clothes, and herself put on a pretty blue dress which she knew her husband liked.

You may fancy how glad this good wife was to see him come home safe and sound, and how the little girl clapped her hands, and laughed with delight, when she saw the pretty toys her father had brought for her. He had much to tell of all the wonderful things he had seen upon the journey, and in the town itself.

"I have brought you a very pretty thing," said he to his wife. "It is called a mirror. Look and tell me what you see inside." He gave to her a plain, white, wooden box, in which, when she opened it, she found a round piece of metal. One side was white like frosted silver, and ornamented with raised figures of birds and flowers; the other was bright as the clearest crystal. Into it the young mother looked with delight and astonishment, for from its depths was looking at her a smiling, happy face.

"What do you see?" again asked the husband, pleased at her astonishment, and glad to show that he had learned something while he had been away.

"I see a pretty woman looking at me, and she moves her lips as if she were speaking, and—dear me, how odd, she has on a blue dress just like mine!"

"Why, it is your own face that you see," said the husband, proud of knowing something that his wife didn't know. "That round piece of metal is called a mirror. In the town everybody has one, although we have not seen them in this country place before."

The wife was charmed with her present, and for a few days could not look into the mirror often enough, for you must remember that this was the first time she had seen a mirror, so of course it was the first time she had ever seen the reflection of her own pretty face. But she considered such a wonderful thing far too precious for everyday use, and soon shut it up in its box again, and put it away carefully among her most valued treasures.

II

Years passed, and the husband and wife still lived happily. The joy of their life was their little daughter, who grew up the very image of her mother, and who was so dutiful and affectionate that everybody loved her. Mindful of her own little passing vanity on finding herself so lovely, the mother kept the mirror carefully hidden away, fearing that the use of it might breed a spirit of pride in her little girl.

She never spoke of it; and as for the father, he had forgotten all about it. So the daughter grew up as simple as the mother had been, and knew nothing of her own good looks, or of the mirror which would have reflected them.

But by and by a sad misfortune came to this happy little family. The kind mother fell sick; and, although her daughter waited upon her day and night, with loving care, she got worse and worse, until at last there was no hope but that she must die.

When she found that she must so soon leave her husband and child, the poor woman felt very sorrowful, grieving for those she was going to leave behind, and most of all for her little daughter.

She called the girl to her and said, "My darling child, you know that I am very sick; soon I must die, and leave your dear father and you alone. When I am gone, promise me that you will look into this mirror every night and every morning. There you will see me, and know that I am still watching over you." With these words she took the mirror from its hiding place and gave it to her daughter. The child promised, with many tears, and so the mother, seeming now calm and resigned, died a short time after.

Now this obedient and dutiful daughter never forgot her mother's last request, but each morning and evening took the mirror from its hiding place, and looked in it long and earnestly. There she saw the bright and smiling vision of her lost mother; not pale and sickly as in her last days, but the beautiful young mother of long ago. To her, at night, she told the story of the trials and difficulties of the day; to her, in the morning, she looked for sympathy and encouragement in whatever might be in store for her.

So day by day she lived as in her mother's sight, striving still to please her as she had done in her lifetime, and careful always to avoid whatever might pain or grieve her.

Her greatest joy was to be able to look in the mirror and say, "Mother, I have been today what you would have me be."

Seeing her every night and morning, without fail, look into the mirror, and seem to hold converse with it, her father at length asked her the reason for her strange behavior.

"Father," she said, "I look in the mirror every day to see my dear mother and to talk with her." Then she told him of her mother's dying wish, and how she had never failed to fulfill it. Touched by so much simplicity, and such faithful, loving obedience, the father shed tears of pity and affection. Nor could he find it in his heart to tell the child that the image she saw in the mirror was but the reflection of her own sweet face, becoming more and more like her dear mother's, day by day.

Nails in the Post

M. F. COWDERY

In this tough story from a Civil War-era school reader, we find another kind of lesson that some homes offer. Here is a father giving his son stern but loving moral instruction.

There was once a farmer who had a son named John, a boy very apt to be thoughtless, and careless about doing what he was told to do.

One day his father said to him, "John, you are so careless and forgetful, that every time you do wrong, I shall drive a nail into this post, to remind you how often you are naughty. And every time you do right I will draw one out." His father did as he said he would, and every day he had one and sometimes a great many nails to drive in, but very seldom one to draw out.

At last John saw that the post was quite covered with nails, and he began to be ashamed of having so many faults. He resolved to be a better boy, and the next day he was so good and industrious that several nails came out. The day after it was the same thing, and so on for a long time, till at length only one nail remained. His father then called him, and said: "Look, John, here is the very last nail, and now I'm going to draw it out. Are you not glad?"

John looked at the post, and then, instead of expressing his joy, as his father expected, he burst into tears. "Why," said the father, "what's the matter? I should think you would be delighted; the nails are all gone."

"Yes," sobbed John, "the *nails* are gone, but the *scars* are there yet."

So it is, dear children, with your faults and bad habits; you may overcome them, you may by degrees cure them, but the scars remain. Now, take my advice, and whenever you find yourselves doing a wrong thing, or getting into a bad habit, stop at once. For every time you give in to it, you drive another nail, and that will leave a *scar* on your soul, even if the nail should be afterwards drawn out.

The Night Wind

EUGENE FIELD

At home that guardian of virtue we call conscience takes root. It talks to us often, even when we don't ask it to.

Have you ever heard the wind go "Yooooo"?
    'Tis a pitiful sound to hear.
It seems to chill you through and through
    With a strange and speechless fear.
It's the voice of the night that broods outside
    When folks should be asleep;
And many and many's the time I've cried
To the darkness that brooded far and wide
    Over the land and the deep:
"Whom do you want, O lonely night,
That you wail the long hours through?"
And the night would say in its ghostly way:
    "Yoo—oo—oo—oo! Yoo—oo—oo—oo!
        Yoo—oo—oo—oo!"

My mother told me long ago
    (When I was a little lad),
That when the night went wailing so,
    Somebody had been bad.
And then, when I was snug in bed,
    Whither I had been sent,
With the blankets drawn up around my head,
I'd think of what my mother'd said,
    And wonder what boy she meant.
"And who's been bad today?" I'd ask
Of the wind that hoarsely blew.
And that voice would say in its awful way:
    "Yoo—oo—oo—oo! Yoo—oo—oo—oo!
        Yoo—oo—oo—oo!"

That this was true I must allow—
    You'll not believe it though!—
Yes, though I'm quite a model now,
    I was not always so.
And if you doubt what things I say,
    Suppose you make the test;
Suppose when you've been bad some day,
And up to bed you're sent away
    From mother and the rest—
Suppose you ask, "Who has been bad?"
And then you'll hear what's true.
For the wind will moan in its ruefullest tone:
    "Yoo—oo—oo—oo! Yoo—oo—oo—oo!
        Yoo—oo—oo—oo!"

Northwest Passage

There is no better place to begin learning about bravery than in the safe confines of home. For many children, the first great adventure is that long, perilous journey up the stairs to bed. Making it can be a first exercise in courage.

1. GOOD NIGHT

When the bright lamp is carried in,
The sunless hours again begin;
O'er all without, in field and lane,
The haunted night returns again.

Now we behold the embers flee
About the firelit hearth; and see
Our faces painted as we pass,
Like pictures, on the window glass.

Must we to bed indeed? Well then,
Let us arise and go like men,
And face with an undaunted tread
The long black passage up to bed.

Farewell, O brother, sister, sire!
O pleasant party round the fire!
The songs you sing, the tales you tell,
Till far tomorrow, fare ye well!

2. SHADOW MARCH

All 'round the house is the jet-black night;
It stares through the windowpane;
It crawls in the corners, hiding from the light,
And it moves with the moving flame.

Now my little heart goes a-beating like a drum,
With the breath of the bogy in my hair;
And all round the candle the crooked shadows come,
And go marching along up the stair.

The shadow of the balusters, the shadow of the lamp,
The shadow of the child that goes to bed—
All the wicked shadows coming, tramp, tramp, tramp,
With the black night overhead.

3. IN PORT

Last, to the chamber where I lie
My fearful footsteps patter nigh,
And come from out the cold and gloom
Into my warm and cheerful room.

There, safe arrived, we turn about
To keep the coming shadows out,
And close the happy door at last
On all the perils that we passed.

Then, when Mama goes by to bed,
She shall come in with tiptoe tread,
And see me lying warm and fast
And in the Land of Nod at last.

The Place of Brotherhood

JEWISH FOLKTALE

This beautiful Jewish story reminds us that home should be the place where we learn about selflessness and how to practice it with those closest to us. King Solomon built the Temple of Israel to house the ark of the covenant in the tenth century B.C.

In the days of King Solomon there lived two brothers who reaped wheat in the fields of Zion. One night, in the dark of the moon, the elder brother gathered several sheaves of his harvest and left it in his brother's field, saying to himself: "My brother has seven children. With so many mouths to feed, he could use some of my bounty." And he went home.

A short time later, the younger brother slipped out of his house, gathered several sheaves of *his* wheat, and carried it into his brother's field, saying to himself: "My brother is all alone, with no one to help him harvest. So I'll share some of my wheat with him."

When the sun rose, each brother was amazed to find he had just as much wheat as before!

The next night they paid each other the same kindness, and still woke to find their stores undiminished.

But on the third night, they met each other as they carried their gifts into each other's fields. Each threw his arms around the other and shed tears of joy for his goodness.

And when Solomon heard of their love, he built the Temple of Israel there on the place of brotherhood.

Plato on Responsibility

FROM THE *CRITO*

In this famous dialogue by Plato, Crito visits his friend Socrates, who has been legally but unjustly imprisoned and condemned to death for "impiety" and "corrupting the youth." The hour when Socrates must drink the poison hemlock is fast approaching, and Crito tries to persuade his friend to escape. Socrates, however, refuses to break the law of Athens. His argument is one of our finest lessons in the principles that must inform both civil obedience and civil disobedience. His decision to die remains one of history's great examples of an individual who believes his first responsibility to his community, his family, and himself is to follow the dictates of reason-directed conscience.

Socrates. Consider the matter in this way: Imagine that I am about to play truant (you may call the proceeding by any name which you like), and the laws and the government come and interrogate me: "Tell us, Socrates," they say; "what are you about? Are you not going by an act of yours to overturn us—the laws, and the whole state, as far as in you lies? Do you imagine that a state can subsist and not be overthrown, in which the decisions of law have no power, but are set aside and trampled upon by individuals?" What will be our answer, Crito, to these and the like words? Anyone, and especially a rhetorician, will have a good deal to say on behalf of the law which requires a sentence to be carried out. He will argue that this law should not be set aside; and shall we reply, "Yes; but the state has injured us and given an unjust sentence"? Suppose I say that?

Crito. Very good, Socrates.

Socrates. "And was that our agreement with you?" The law would answer; "Or were you to abide by the sentence of the state?" And if I were to express my astonishment at their words, the law would probably add: "Answer, Socrates, instead of opening your eyes—you are in the habit of asking and answering questions. Tell us—What complaint have you to make against us which justifies you in attempting to destroy us and the state? In the first place did we not bring you into existence? Your father married your mother by our aid and begat you. Say whether you have any objection to urge against those of us who regulate marriage?" None, I should reply. "Or against those of us who after birth regulate the nurture and education of children, in which you also were trained? Were not the laws, which have the charge of education, right in commanding your father to train you in music and gymnastics?" Right, I should reply. "Well then, since you were brought into the world and nurtured and educated by us, can you deny in the first place that you are our child and slave, as your fathers were before you? And if this is true you are not on equal terms with us; nor can you think that you have a right to do to us what we are doing to you. Would you have any right to strike or revile or do any other evil to your father or your master, if you had one, because you have been struck or reviled by him, or received some other evil at his hands?—You would not say this? And because we think right to destroy you, do you think that you have any right to destroy us in return, and your country as far as in you lies? Will you, O professor of true virtue, pretend that you are justified in this? Has a philosopher like you failed to discover that our country is more to be valued and higher and holier far than mother or father or any ancestor, and more to be regarded in the eyes of the gods and of men of understanding? Also to be soothed, and gently and reverently entreated when angry, even more than a father, and either to be persuaded, or if not persuaded, to be obeyed? And when we are punished by her, whether with imprisonment or stripes, the punishment is to be endured in silence; and if she leads us to wounds or death in battle, thither we follow as is right; neither may anyone yield or retreat or leave his rank, but whether in battle or in a court of law, or in any other place, he must do what his city and his country order him; or he must change their view of what is just: and if he may do no violence to his father or mother, much less may he do violence to his country." What answer shall we make to this, Crito? Do the laws speak truly, or do they not?

Crito. I think that they do.

Socrates. Then the laws will say, "Consider, Socrates, if we are speaking truly that in your present attempt you are going to do us an injury. For, having brought you into the world, and nurtured and educated you, and given you and every other citizen a share in every good which we had to give, we further proclaim to any Athenian by the liberty which we allow him, that if he does not like us when he has become of age and has seen the ways of the city, and made our acquaintance, he may go where he pleases and take his goods with him. None of us laws will forbid him or interfere with him. Anyone who does not like us and the city, and who wants to emigrate to a colony or to any other city, may go where he likes, retaining his property. But he who has experience of the manner in which we order justice and administer the state, and still remains, has entered into an implied contract that he will do as we command him. And he who disobeys us is, as we maintain, thrice wrong; first, because in disobeying us he is disobeying his parents; secondly, because we are the authors of his education; thirdly, because he has made an agreement with us that he will duly obey our commands; and he neither obeys them nor convinces us that our commands are unjust; and we do not rudely impose them, but give him the alternative of obeying or convincing us; that is what we offer, and he does neither.

"These are the sort of accusations to which, as we were saying, you, Socrates, will be exposed if you accomplish your intentions; you, above all other Athenians." Suppose now I ask, why I rather than anybody else? They will justly retort upon me that I above all other men have acknowledged the agreement. "There is clear proof," they will say, "Socrates, that we and the city were not displeasing to you. Of all Athenians you have been the most constant resident in the city, which, as you never leave, you may be supposed to love. For you never went out of the city either to see the games, except once when you went to the Isthmus, or to any other place unless when you were on military service; nor did you travel as other men do. Nor had you any curiosity to know other states or their laws: your affections did not go beyond us and our state; we were your special favorites, and you acquiesced in our government of you; and here in this city you begat your children, which is a proof of your satisfaction. Moreover, you might in the course of the trial, if you had liked, have fixed the penalty at banishment; the state which refuses to let you go now would have let you go then. But you pretended that you preferred death to exile, and that you were not unwilling to die. And now you have forgotten these fine sentiments, and pay no respect to us the laws, of whom you are the destroyer; and are doing what only a miserable slave would do, running away and turning your back upon the compacts and agreements which you made as a citizen. And first of all answer this very question: Are we right in saying that you agreed to be governed according to us in deed, and not in word only? Is that true or not?" How shall we answer, Crito? Must we not assent?

Crito. We cannot help it, Socrates.

Socrates. Then will they not say: "You, Socrates, are breaking the covenants and agreements which you made with us at your leisure, not in any haste or under any compulsion or deception, but after you have had seventy years to think of them, during which time you were at liberty to leave the city, if we were not to your mind, or if our covenants appeared to you to be unfair. You had your choice, and might have gone either to Lacedaemon or Crete, both which states are often praised by you for their good government, or to some other Hellenic or foreign state. Whereas you, above all other Athenians, seemed to be so fond of the state, or, in other words, of us her laws (and who would care about a state which has no laws?), that you never stirred out of her; the halt, the blind, the maimed were not more stationary in her than you were. And now you run away and forsake your agreements. Not so, Socrates, if you will take our advice; do not make yourself ridiculous by escaping out of the city.

"For just consider, if you transgress and err in this sort of way, what good will you do either to yourself or to your friends? That your friends will be driven into exile and deprived of citizenship, or will lose their property, is tolerably certain; and you yourself, if you fly to one of the neighboring cities, as, for example, Thebes or Megara, both of which are well governed, will come to them as an enemy, Socrates, and their government will be against you, and all patriotic citizens will cast an evil eye upon you as a subverter of the laws, and you will confirm in the minds of the judges the justice of their own condemnation of you. For he who is a corrupter of the laws is more than likely to be a corrupter of the young and foolish portion of mankind. Will you then flee from well-ordered cities and virtuous men? And is existence worth having on these terms? Or will you go to them without shame, and talk to them, Socrates? And what will you say to them? What you say here about virtue and justice and institutions and laws being the best things among men? Would that be decent of you? Surely not. But if you go away from well-governed states to Crito's friends in Thessaly, where there is great disorder and license, they will be charmed to hear the tale of your escape from prison, set off with ludicrous particulars of the manner in which you were wrapped in a goatskin or some other disguise, and metamorphosed as the manner is of runaways; but will there be no one to remind you that in your old age you were not ashamed to violate the most sacred laws from a miserable desire of a little more life? Perhaps not, if you keep them in a good temper; but if they are out of temper you will hear many degrading things; you will live, but how?—as the flatterer of all men, and the servant of all men; and doing what?—eating and drinking in Thessaly, having gone abroad in order that you may get a dinner. And where will be your fine sentiments about justice and virtue? Say that you wish to live for the sake of your children—you want to bring them up and educate them—will you take them into Thessaly and deprive them of Athenian citizenship? Is this the benefit which you will confer upon them? Or are you under the impression that they will be better cared for and educated here if you are still alive, although absent from them; for your friends will take care of them? Do you fancy that if you are an inhabitant of Thessaly they will take care of them, and if you are an inhabitant of the other world that they will not take care of them? Nay; but if they who call themselves friends are good for anything, they will—to be sure they will.

"Listen, then, Socrates, to us who have brought you up. Think not of life and children first, and of justice afterward, but of justice first, that you may be justified before the princes of the world below. For neither will you nor any that belong to you be happier or holier or juster in this life, or happier in another, if you do as Crito bids. Now you depart in innocence, a sufferer and not a doer of evil; a victim, not of the laws but of men. But if you go forth, returning evil for evil, and injury for injury, breaking the covenants and agreements which you have made with us, and wronging those whom you ought least of all to wrong, that is to say, yourself, your friends, your country, and us, we shall be angry with you while you live, and our brethren, the laws in the world below, will receive you as an enemy; for they will know that you have done your best to destroy us. Listen, then, to us and not to Crito."

This, dear Crito, is the voice which I seem to hear murmuring in my ears, like the sound of the flute in the ears of the mystic; that voice, I say, is humming in my ears, and prevents me from hearing any other. And I know that anything more which you may say will be vain. Yet speak, if you have anything to say.

Crito. I have nothing to say, Socrates.

Socrates. Leave me then, Crito, to fulfill the will of God, and to follow whither he leads.

Prayer for Home and Family

This beautiful prayer sums up, I think, what family life should be. I read it for the first time recently and hope to make it familiar in the Bennett home.

Lord, behold our family here assembled. We thank Thee for this place in which we dwell; for the love that unites us; for the peace accorded us this day; for the hope with which we expect the morrow; for the health, the work, the food, and the bright skies, that make our lives delightful; for our friends in all parts of the earth.

Let peace abound in our small company. Purge out of every heart the lurking grudge. Give us grace and strength to forbear and to persevere. Offenders, give us the grace to accept and to forgive offenders. Forgetful ourselves, help us to bear cheerfully the forgetfulness of others.

Give us courage and gaiety and the quiet mind. Spare to us our friends, soften to us our enemies. Bless us, if it may be, in all our innocent endeavors. If it may not, give us the strength to encounter that which is to come, that we may be brave in peril, constant in tribulation, temperate in wrath, and in all changes of fortune, and down to the gates of death, loyal and loving one to another.

As the clay to the potter, as the windmill to the wind, as children of their sire, we beseech of Thee this help and mercy for Christ's sake.

The Prince's Happy Heart

FOLKTALE

A close-knit and loving home is worth more than a kingdom, as the little prince discovers in this story.

I

Once upon a time there was a little Prince in a country far away from here. He was one of the happiest little Princes who ever lived. All day long he laughed and sang and played. His voice was as sweet as music. His footsteps brought joy wherever he went. Everyone thought that this was due to magic. Hung about the Prince's neck on a gold chain was a wonderful heart. It was made of gold and set with precious stones.

The godmother of the little Prince had given the heart to him when he was very small. She had said as she slipped it over his curly head: "To wear this happy heart will keep the Prince happy always. Be careful that he does not lose it."

All the people who took care of the little Prince were very careful to see that the chain of the happy heart was clasped. But one day they found the little Prince in his garden, very sad and sorrowful. His face was wrinkled into an ugly frown.

"Look!" he said, and he pointed to his neck. Then they saw what had happened.

The happy heart was gone. No one could find it, and each day the little Prince grew more sorrowful. At last they missed him. He had gone, himself, to look for the lost happy heart that he needed so much.

II

The little Prince searched all day. He looked in the city streets and along the country roads. He looked in the shops and in the doors of the houses where rich people lived. Nowhere could he find the heart that he had lost. At last it was almost night. He was very tired and hungry. He had never before walked so far, or felt so unhappy.

Just as the sun was setting the little Prince came to a tiny house. It was very poor and weather-stained. It stood on the edge of the forest. But a bright light streamed from the window. So he lifted the latch, as a Prince may, and went inside.

There was a mother rocking a baby to sleep. The father was reading a story out loud. The little daughter was setting the table for supper. A boy of the Prince's own age was tending the fire. The mother's dress was old. There were to be only porridge and potatoes for supper. The fire was very small. But all the family were as happy as the little Prince wanted to be. Such smiling faces and light feet the children had. How sweet the mother's voice was!

"Won't you have supper with us?" they begged. They did not seem to notice the Prince's ugly frown.

"Where are your happy hearts?" he asked them.

"We don't know what you mean," the boy and the girl said.

"Why," the Prince said, "to laugh and be as happy as you are, one has to wear a gold chain about one's neck. Where are yours?"

Oh, how the children laughed! "We don't need to wear gold hearts," they said. "We all love each other so much, and we play that this house is a castle and that we have turkey and ice cream for supper. After supper mother will tell us stories. That is all we need to make us happy."

"I will stay with you for supper," said the little Prince.

So he had supper in the tiny house that was a castle. And he played that the porridge and potato were turkey and ice cream. He helped to wash the dishes, and then they all sat about the fire. They played that the small fire was a great one, and listened to fairy stories that the mother told. All at once the little Prince began to smile. His laugh was just as merry as it used to be. His voice was again as sweet as music.

He had a very pleasant time, and then the boy walked part of the way home with him. When they were almost to the palace gates, the Prince said:

"It's very strange, but I feel just exactly as if I had found my happy heart."

The boy laughed. "Why, you have," he said. "Only now you are wearing it inside."

The Silent Couple

FOLKTALE

This tale appears in different versions all over the world, from Sri Lanka to Scotland. This version warns us that pettiness can cause us to forget our obligations.

There was once a young man who was said to be the most pigheaded fellow in town, and a young woman who was said to be the most muleheaded maiden, and of course they somehow managed to fall in love and be married. After the wedding ceremony, they had a grand feast at their new house, which lasted all day.

Finally all the friends and relatives could eat no more, and one by one they went home. The bride and groom collapsed from exhaustion, and were just getting ready to take off their shoes and relax, when the husband noticed that the last guest to leave had failed to close the door.

"My dear," he said, "would you mind getting up and shutting the door? There's a draft coming in."

"Why should I shut it?" yawned the wife. "I've been on my feet all day, and I just sat down. You shut it."

"So that's the way it's going to be!" snapped the husband. "Just as soon as you get the ring on your finger, you turn into a lazy good-for-nothing!"

"How dare you!" shouted the bride. "We haven't even been married a day, and already you're calling me names and ordering me around! I should have known this is the kind of husband you'd turn out to be!"

"Nag, nag, nag," grumbled the husband. "Must I listen to your complaining forever?"

"And must I always listen to your carping and whining?" asked the wife.

They sat glaring at each other for a full five minutes. Then an idea popped into the bride's head.

"My dear," she said, "neither of us wants to shut the door, and both of us are tired of hearing the other's voice. So I propose a contest. The one who speaks first must get up and close the door."

"It's the best idea I've heard all day," replied the husband. "Let us begin now."

So they made themselves comfortable, each on a chair, and sat face-to-face without saying a word.

They had been that way for about two hours when a couple of thieves with a cart passed by and saw the open door. They crept into the house, which seemed perfectly deserted, and began to steal everything they could lay their hands on. They took tables and chairs, pulled paintings off the walls, even rolled up carpets. But the newlyweds neither spoke nor moved.

"I can't believe this," thought the husband. "They'll take everything we own, and she won't make a sound."

"Why doesn't he call for help?" the wife asked herself. "Is he just going to sit there while they steal whatever they want?"

Eventually the thieves noticed the silent, motionless couple and, mistaking them for wax figures, stripped them of their jewelry, watches, and wallets. But neither husband nor wife uttered a sound.

The robbers hurried away with their loot, and the newlyweds sat through the night. At dawn a policeman walked by and, noticing the open door, stuck in his head to ask if everything was all right. But, of course, he couldn't get an answer out of the silent couple.

"Now, see here!" he yelled. "I'm an officer of the law! Who are you? Is this your house? What happened to all your furniture?" And still getting no response, he raised his hands to box the man's ears.

"Don't you dare!" cried the wife, jumping to her feet. "That's my new husband, and if you lay a finger on him, you'll have to answer to me!"

"I won!" yelled the husband, clapping his hands. "Now go and close the door."

Simon's Father

GUY DE MAUPASSANT

This nineteenth-century story of a boy without a father has truths for all times, perhaps most poignantly for the early twenty-first century, when fatherlessness is epidemic. Little boys want to be men, but they need good men to show them how. The lucky boys have such men as fathers.

Noon had just struck. The school door opened and the youngsters tumbled out, rolling over each other in their haste to get out quickly. But instead of promptly dispersing and going home to dinner as was their daily wont, they stopped a few paces off, broke up into knots, and set to whispering.

The fact was that that morning Simon, the son of La Blanchotte, had, for the first time, attended school.

They had all of them in their families heard talk of La Blanchotte; and, although in public she was welcome enough, the mothers among themselves treated her with compassion of a somewhat disdainful kind, which the children had caught without in the least knowing why.

As for Simon himself, they did not know him, for he never went abroad, and did not go galloping about with them through the streets of the village or along the banks of the river. Therefore, they loved him but little; and it was with a certain delight, mingled with considerable astonishment, that they met and that they recited to each other this phrase, set afoot by a lad of fourteen or fifteen who appeared to know all, all about it, so sagaciously did he wink. "You know . . . Simon . . . well, he has no father."

La Blanchotte's son appeared in his turn upon the threshold of the school.

He was seven or eight years old. He was rather pale, very neat, with a timid and almost awkward manner.

He was on the point of making his way back to his mother's house when the groups of his schoolfellows perpetually whispering and watching him with the mischievous and heartless eyes of children bent upon playing a nasty trick, gradually surrounded him and ended by enclosing him altogether. There he stood fixed amidst them, surprised and embarrassed, not understanding what they were going to do with him. But the lad who had brought the news, puffed up with the success he had met with already, demanded, "How do you name yourself, you?"

He answered, "Simon."

"Simon what?" retorted the other.

The child, altogether bewildered, repeated, "Simon."

The lad shouted at him, "One is named Simon something . . . that is not a name . . . Simon indeed."

And he, on the brink of tears, replied for the third time, "I am named Simon."

The urchins fell a-laughing. The lad triumphantly lifted up his voice. "You can see plainly that he has no father."

A deep silence ensued. The children were dumbfounded by this extraordinary, impossible monstrous thing—a boy who had not a father; they looked upon him as a phenomenon, an unnatural being, and they felt that contempt, until then inexplicable, of their mothers for La Blanchotte grow upon them. As for Simon, he had propped himself against a tree to avoid falling and he remained as though struck to the earth by an irreparable disaster. He sought to explain, but he could think of no answer for them, to deny this horrible charge that he had no father. At last he shouted at them quite recklessly, "Yes, I have one."

"Where is he?" demanded the boy.

Simon was silent. He did not know. The children roared, tremendously excited; and these sons of toil, most nearly related to animals, experienced that cruel craving which animates the fowls of a farmyard to destroy one among themselves as soon as it is wounded. Simon suddenly espied a little neighbor, the son of a widow, whom he had always seen, as he himself was to be seen, quite alone with his mother.

"And no more have you," he said, "no more have you a father."

"Yes," replied the other, "I have one."

"Where is he?" rejoined Simon.

"He is dead," declared the brat with superb dignity, "he is in the cemetery, is my father."

A murmur of approval rose amidst the scapegraces, as if this fact of possessing a father dead in a cemetery had caused their comrade to grow big enough to crush the other one who had no father at all. And these rogues, whose fathers were for the most part evildoers, drunkards, thieves, and ill-treaters of their wives, hustled each other as they pressed closer and closer, as though they, the legitimate ones, would stifle in their pressure one who was beyond the law.

He who chanced to be next to Simon suddenly put his tongue out at him with a waggish air and shouted at him, "No father! No father!"

Simon seized him by the hair with both hands and set to work to demolish his legs with kicks, while he bit his cheek ferociously. A tremendous struggle ensued between the two combatants, and Simon found himself beaten, torn, bruised, rolled on the ground in the middle of the ring of applauding vagabonds. As he arose, mechanically brushing his little shirt all covered with dust with his hand, someone shouted at him, "Go and tell your father."

He then felt a great sinking in his heart. They were stronger than he was, they had beaten him and he had no answer to give them, for he knew well that it was true that he had no father. Full of pride he attempted for some moments to struggle against the tears which were suffocating him. He had a choking fit, and then without cries he commenced to weep with great sobs which shook him incessantly. Then a ferocious joy broke out among his enemies, and, naturally, just as with savages in their fearful festivals, they took each other by the hand and set about dancing in a circle about him as they repeated as a refrain, "No father! No father!"

But Simon quite suddenly ceased sobbing. Frenzy overtook him. There were stones under his feet. He picked them up and with all his strength hurled them at his tormentors. Two or three were struck and rushed off yelling, and so formidable did he appear that the rest became panic-stricken. Cowards, as a crowd always is in the presence of an exasperated man, they broke up and fled. Left alone, the little thing without a father set off running toward the fields, for a recollection had been awakened which brought his soul to a great determination. He made up his mind to drown himself in the river.

He remembered, in fact, that eight days before a poor devil who begged for his livelihood, had thrown himself into the water because he had no more money. Simon had been there when they had fished him out again; and the sight of the fellow, who usually seemed to him so miserable, and ugly, had then struck him—his pale cheeks, his long drenched beard, and his open eyes being full of calm. The bystanders had said, "He is dead."

And someone had said, "He is quite happy now."

And Simon wished to drown himself also because he had no father, just like the wretched being who had no money.

He reached the neighborhood of the water and watched it flowing. Some fishes were sporting briskly in the clear stream and occasionally made a little bound and caught the flies flying on the surface. He stopped crying in order to watch them, for their housewifery interested him vastly. But, at intervals, as in the changes of a tempest, altering suddenly from tremendous gusts of wind, which snap off the trees and then lose themselves in the horizon, this thought would return to him with intense pain, "I am about to drown myself because I have no father."

It was very warm and fine weather. The pleasant sunshine warmed the grass. The water shone like a mirror. And Simon enjoyed some minutes the happiness of that languor which follows weeping, in which he felt very desirous of falling asleep there upon the grass in the warmth.

A little green frog leapt from under his feet. He endeavored to catch it. It escaped him. He followed it and lost it three times following. At last he caught it by one of its hind legs and began to laugh as he saw the efforts the creature made to escape. It gathered itself up on its large legs and then with a violent spring suddenly stretched them out as stiff as two bars; while, its eye wide open in its round, golden circle, it beat the air with its front limbs which worked as though they were hands. It reminded him of a toy made with straight slips of wood nailed zigzag one on the other, which by a similar movement regulated the exercise of the little soldiers stuck thereon. Then he thought of his home and next of his mother, and overcome by a great sorrow he again began to weep. His limbs trembled; and he placed himself on his knees and said his prayers as before going to bed. But he was unable to finish them, for such hurried and violent sobs overtook him that he was completely overwhelmed. He thought no more, he no longer saw anything around him and was wholly taken up in crying.

Suddenly a heavy hand was placed upon his shoulder, and a rough voice asked him, "What is it that causes you so much grief, my fine fellow?"

Simon turned 'round. A tall workman with a black beard and hair all curled, was staring at him good-naturedly. He answered with his eyes and throat full of tears, "They have beaten me . . . because . . . I . . . have no . . . father . . . no father."

"What!" said the man smiling, "why, everybody has one."

The child answered painfully amidst his spasms of grief, "But I . . . I . . . I have none."

Then the workman became serious. He had recognized La Blanchotte's son, and although but recently come to the neighborhood he had a vague idea of her history.

"Well," said he, "console yourself, my boy, and come with me home to your mother. They will give you . . . a father."

And so they started on the way, the big one holding the little one by the hand, and the man smiled afresh, for he was not sorry to see this Blanchotte, who was, it was said, one of the prettiest girls of the countryside, and, perhaps, he said to himself, at the bottom of his heart, that a lass who had erred might very well err again.

They arrived in front of a little and very neat white house.

"There it is," exclaimed the child, and he cried "Mamma."

A woman appeared and the workman instantly left off smiling, for he at once perceived that there was no more fooling to be done with the tall pale girl who stood austerely at her door as though to defend from one man the threshold of that house where she had already been betrayed by another. Intimidated, his cap in his hand, he stammered out, "See, madam, I have brought back your little boy, who had lost himself near the river."

But Simon flung his arms about his mother's neck and told her, as he again began to cry, "No, Mamma, I wished to drown myself, because the others had beaten me . . . had beaten me . . . because I have no father."

A burning redness covered the young woman's cheeks, and, hurt to the quick, she embraced her child passionately, while the tears coursed down her face. The man, much moved, stood there, not knowing how to get away. But Simon suddenly ran to him and said, "Will you be my father?"

A deep silence ensued. La Blanchotte, dumb and tortured with shame, leaned herself against the wall, both her hands upon her heart. The child, seeing that no answer was made him, replied, "If you do not wish it, I shall return to drown myself."

The workman took the matter as a jest and answered laughing, "Why, yes, I wish it certainly."

"What is your name, then?" went on the child, "so that I may tell the others when they wish to know your name?"

"Phillip," answered the man.

Simon was silent a moment so that he might get the name well into his head; then he stretched out his arms quite consoled as he said, "Well, then, Phillip, you are my father."

The workman, lifting him from the ground, kissed him hastily on both cheeks, and then made off very quickly with great strides.

When the child returned to school next day he was received with a spiteful laugh, and at the end of school when the lads were on the point of recommencing, Simon threw these words at their heads as he would have done a stone, "He is named Phillip, my father."

Yells of delight burst out from all sides.

"Phillip who? . . . Phillip what? What on earth is Phillip? Where did you pick up your Phillip?"

Simon answered nothing; and immovable in faith he defied them with his eye, ready to be martyred rather than fly before them. The schoolmaster came to his rescue and he returned home to his mother.

During three months, the tall workman, Phillip, frequently passed by La Blanchotte's house, and sometimes he made bold to speak to her when he saw her sewing near the window. She answered him civilly, always sedately, never joking with him, nor permitting him to enter her house. Notwithstanding which, being, like all men, a bit of a coxcomb, he imagined that she was often rosier than usual when she chatted with him.

But a fallen reputation is so difficult to recover and always remains so fragile that, in spite of the shy reserve La Blanchotte maintained, they already gossiped in the neighborhood.

As for Simon, he loved his new father much, and walked with him nearly every evening when the day's work was done. He went regularly to school and mixed with great dignity with his schoolfellows without ever answering them back.

One day, however, the lad who had first attacked him said to him, "You have lied. You have not a father named Phillip."

"Why do you say that?" demanded Simon, much disturbed.

The youth rubbed his hands. He replied, "Because if you had one he would be your mamma's husband."

Simon was confused by the truth of this reasoning, nevertheless he retorted, "He is my father all the same."

"That can very well be," exclaimed the urchin with a sneer, "but that is not being your father altogether."

La Blanchotte's little one bowed his head and went off dreaming in the direction of the forge belonging to old Loizon, where Phillip worked.

This forge was as though entombed in trees. It was very dark there, the red glare of a formidable furnace alone lit up with great flashes by five blacksmiths, who hammered upon their anvils with a terrible din. They were standing enveloped in flame, like demons, their eyes fixed on the red-hot iron they were pounding; and their dull ideas rose and fell with their hammers.

Simon entered without being noticed and went quietly to pluck his friend by the sleeve. He turned himself 'round. All at once the work came to a standstill and all the men looked on very attentive. Then, in the midst of this unaccustomed silence, rose the little slender pipe of Simon; "Phillip, explain to me what the lad at La Michande has just told me, that you are not altogether my father."

"And why that?" asked the smith.

The child replied with all its innocence, "Because you are not my mamma's husband."

No one laughed. Phillip remained standing, leaning his forehead upon the back of his great hands, which supported the handle of his hammer standing upright upon the anvil. He mused. His four companions watched him, and, quite a tiny mite among these giants, Simon anxiously waited. Suddenly, one of the smiths, answering to the sentiment of all, said to Phillip, "La Blanchotte is all the same a good and honest girl, and stalwart and steady in spite of her misfortune, and one who would make a worthy wife for an honest man."

"That is true," remarked the three others.

The smith continued, "Is it this girl's fault if she has fallen? She had been promised marriage and I know more than one who is much respected today, and who sinned every bit as much."

"That is true," responded the three men in chorus. He resumed, "How hard she has toiled, poor thing, to educate her lad all alone, and how much she has wept since she no longer goes out, save to go to church, God only knows."

"This also is true," said the others.

Then no more was heard than the bellows which fanned the fire of the furnace. Phillip hastily bent himself down to Simon. "Go and tell your mamma that I shall come to speak to her."

Then he pushed the child out by the shoulders. He returned to his work and with a single blow the five hammers again fell upon their anvils. Thus they wrought the iron until nightfall, strong, powerful, happy, like hammers satisfied. But just as the great bell of a cathedral resounds upon feast days above the jingling of the other bells, so Phillip's hammer, dominating the noise of the others, clanged second after second with a deafening uproar. And he, his eye on fire, plied his trade vigorously, erect amid the sparks.

The sky was full of stars as he knocked at La Blanchotte's door. He had his Sunday blouse on, a fresh shirt, and his beard was trimmed. The young woman showed herself upon the threshold and said in a grieved tone, "It is ill to come thus when night has fallen, Mr. Phillip."

He wished to answer, but stammered and stood confused before her.

She resumed, "And still you understand quite well that it will not do that I should be talked about any more."

Then he said all at once, "What does that matter to me, if you will be my wife!"

No voice replied to him, but he believed that he heard in the shadow of the room the sound of a body that sank down. He entered very quickly; and Simon, who had gone to his bed, distinguished the sound of a kiss and some words that his mother said very softly. Then he suddenly found himself lifted up by the hands of his friend, who, holding him at the length of his herculean arms, exclaimed to him, "You will tell them, your schoolfellows, that your father is Phillip Remy, the blacksmith, and that he will pull the ears of all who do you any harm."

On the morrow, when the school was full and lessons were about to begin, little Simon stood up quite pale with trembling lips. "My father," said he in a clear voice, "is Phillip Remy, the blacksmith, and he has promised to box the ears of all who do me any harm."

This time no one laughed any longer, for he was very well known, was Phillip Remy, the blacksmith, and was a father of whom anyone in the world would have been proud.

What a Baby Costs

EDGAR GUEST

It is never too early to begin impressing upon our children, by both word and deed, the responsibilities of parenthood. Part of the job of raising children is raising them to be successful parents themselves.

"How much do babies cost?" said he
The other night upon my knee;
And then I said: "They cost a lot;
A lot of watching by a cot,
A lot of sleepless hours and care,
A lot of heartache and despair,
A lot of fear and trying dread,
And sometimes many tears are shed
In payment for our babies small,
But every one is worth it all.

"For babies people have to pay
A heavy price from day to day—

There is no way to get one cheap.
Why, sometimes when they're fast asleep
You have to get up in the night
And go and see that they're all right.
But what they cost in constant care
And worry, does not half compare
With what they bring of joy and bliss—
You'd pay much more for just a kiss.

"Who buys a baby has to pay
A portion of the bill each day;
He has to give his time and thought
Unto the little one he's bought.
He has to stand a lot of pain
Inside his heart and not complain;
And pay with lonely days and sad
For all the happy hours he's had.
All this a baby cost, and yet
His smile is worth it all, you bet."

Why the Baby Says "Goo"

ADAPTED FROM A RETELLING
BY GILBERT L. WILSON

Here is one of the fundamental truths of family life: Baby changes everything.

In a village near the mountains lived an Indian chief. He was a brave man and had fought in many battles. No one in the tribe had won more battles than he.

Strange folk were then in the land. Fierce ice giants came out of the North and carried people away. Wicked witches dwelt in caves, and in the mountains lived the Mikumwess, magic little people.

But the chief feared none of them. He fought the ice giants and made them go back to their home in the North. Some of the witches he killed. Others he drove from the land.

Everybody loved the chief. He was so brave and good that the villagers thought there was no one like him anywhere.

But when he had driven out all the giants, the chief grew

vain. He began to think he was the most important person in the world.

"I can conquer anyone," he boasted. "And no one tells me what to do."

When his wife heard how the great chief boasted, she smiled. "My husband *is* wonderful," she said, "but there is one who is mightier than he. There is one whom even he must obey."

When the chief heard her say this, he asked, "Who is this wonderful one? Where is he?"

His wife smiled again. "You already know him," she said. "His name is Wasis."

Now who do you think Wasis was? He was their own plump little Baby. In the middle of the floor he sat, crowing to himself and sucking a piece of maple sugar. He looked very sweet and contented.

Now the chief, like all vain people, thought he knew everything. He thought, of course, that the little Baby would obey him. So he smiled and said to little Wasis, "Baby, come to me!"

But the Baby smiled back and went on sucking his maple sugar.

The chief was surprised. The villagers always did what he bade them. He could not understand why the little Baby did not obey him, but he smiled and said again to little Wasis, *"Baby, come to me!"*

The little Baby smiled back and sucked his maple sugar as before.

The chief was astonished. No one had ever dared disobey him before. He grew angry. He frowned at little Wasis and roared out, "BABY, COME TO ME!"

But little Wasis opened his mouth and burst out crying and screaming. The chief had never heard such awful sounds. Even the ice giants did not scream so terribly.

The chief was more and more astonished. He could not think why such a little Baby would not obey him.

"Wonderful!" he said. "All other men fear me. But this little Baby shouts back war cries. Perhaps I can overcome him with my magic."

He took out his medicine bag and shook it at the little Baby. He danced magic dances. He sang wonderful songs.

Little Wasis smiled and watched the chief with big round eyes. He thought it all very funny. And all the time he sucked his maple sugar.

The chief danced until he was tired out. Sweat ran down his face. Red paint oozed over his cheeks and neck. The feathers in his headdress had fallen down.

At last he sat down. He was too tired to dance any longer.

"Did I not tell you that Wasis is mightier than you?" asked his wife. "No one is mightier than the Baby. He always rules the wigwam. Everybody loves him and obeys him."

"It is even so," sighed the chief, as he went out of the wigwam. But as he went he could hear little Wasis talking to himself on the floor.

"Goo, goo, goo!" he crowed, as he sucked his maple sugar.

Now, when you hear the Baby saying, "Goo, goo, goo," you will know what it means. It is his war cry. He is happy because he remembers the time when he made the great chief understand who really rules the wigwam.

Acknowledgments

For permission to reprint copyrighted material, grateful acknowledgment is made to the following publishers, authors, and agents:

"F. Scott Fitzgerald to His Daughter" reprinted from *F. Scott Fitzgerald: The Crackup*. Copyright 1945 by New Directions Publishing Corp. Reprinted by permission of New Directions Publishing Corp.

The editor also gratefully acknowledges the endeavors of scholars and collectors such as James Baldwin, Jesse Lyman Hurlbut, and Andrew Lang, who in a past age devoted their energies to preserving some of the best of our heritage, and whose works have supplied this volume with many truly great stories.

Reasonable care has been taken to trace ownership and, when necessary, obtain permission for each selection included.

William J. Bennett served as Director of the Office of National Drug Control Policy under President George Bush and as Secretary of Education and Chairman of the National Endowment for the Humanities under President Reagan. He holds a bachelor of arts degree in philosophy from Williams College, a doctorate in political philosophy from the University of Texas, and a law degree from Harvard. Dr. Bennett is currently a codirector of Empower America, and a Distinguished Fellow in Cultural Policy Studies at the Heritage Foundation. He is also chairman and cofounder of K12, an Internet-based elementary and secondary school. He, his wife Elayne, and their two sons, John and Joseph, live in Chevy Chase, Maryland.

Through inspiring stories and touching narrative, learn to discover the true leader you were meant to be.

William J. Bennett's classic collections have become directional guides for the morality of today's family. This anthology of character building stories from history, the Bible, mythology, poetry, and modern fiction will inspire families to contemplate and discuss the qualities of leadership.

STORIES FROM THE BOOK OF VIRTUES

Life's Virtues

Virtues of
Leadership

William J. Bennett